MEDICAL SCHOOL ADMISSIONS:

··

The Insider's Guide

5th Revised Edition

John A. Zebala, M.D.
Daniel B. Jones, M.D.
Stephanie B. Jones, M.D.

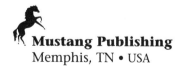
Mustang Publishing
Memphis, TN • USA

Library of Congress Cataloging in Publication Data
Zebala, John A., 1965-
    Medical school admissions : the insider's guide / John A. Zebala,
Daniel B. Jones, Stephanie B. Jones. – 5th rev. ed.
        p.   cm.
    Includes bibliographical references (p.   ).
    ISBN 0-914457-94-2 (paper : alk. paper)
    1. Medical colleges--United States--Admissions. 2. Medical
colleges--United States--Entrance requirements. I. Jones, Daniel
B., 1965- . II. Jones, Stephanie B. (Stephanie Brickner)
R838.4.Z42 1999
610'.71'173--dc21   99-23877
                                                                        CIP

Printed on acid-free paper.
10 9 8 7 6 5 4 3 2 1

Wherever the art

of medicine is

loved, there is also

love of humanity.

— Hippocrates

ACKNOWLEDGMENTS

*T*HIS BOOK IS DEDICATED to our undergraduate and graduate friends, without whose knowledge, inspiration, and sometimes irritation it never would have been written.

We would also like to thank the many Deans of Admission who gave thoughtful commentary on previous editions.

Special thanks also to the students accepted at Cornell University Medical College, Johns Hopkins, Yale, Harvard, UCLA, University of Pennsylvania, Columbia, Washington University, U.T. Southwestern, and elsewhere who contributed their successful essays. These students include (but are not limited to) Wendell Danforth, John Linsalata, Matt Pease, Jeff Budoff, Hal Baker, Dan Medalie, Karl Illig, Daniel Javit, Fred Lee, Perry Sutaria, and Alfonso Torres.

Dan and Stephanie would also like to dedicate this edition to Ryan, Leah, and Cara.

Most important, we would like to thank our parents, who supported us throughout the admissions process not too long ago.

John A. Zebala
Daniel B. Jones
Stephanie B. Jones

F O R E W O R D

··

S INCE THE FIRST EDITION OF THIS BOOK in 1989, many
things about medical school admissions have changed. The most
prominent development has been the increased number of applicants, which grew from 26,917 in 1989 to a peak of 46,968 in 1996.
During all this time, the competition became more keen, because the
number of first-year positions remained nearly constant at about 16,100.
By 1998, the number of applicants was down 12% to 41,003, but the
competition did not let up.

The academic qualifications of the applicants have continued to
improve over time. Those who applied for entry in 1998 had an average
GPA of 3.4 and an average total score on the MCAT of 26.7. Successful
applicants that year had even better marks, with an average GPA of 3.6
and average total MCAT of 29.9. Both of these values are slightly higher
for successful applicants than they had been in 1996, when the number
of applicants was at a record high.

Thus, while the total number of applicants decreased from 1996 to
1998 and the competition relaxed numerically, from an academic perspective the competition has remained at all-time highly intense levels.
As a result, knowing how to navigate the key steps in the application
and interview process has never been more important.

The growing number of applicants has not been evenly distributed
among various groups. While the percentage of female applicants rose
from 30% in 1980 to 43% in 1998, the number of underrepresented minority applicants, particularly African-American men, has not kept
pace, and underrepresentation of some minority groups has worsened.

Meanwhile, the medical profession has been changing, too. Medicine is more exhilarating than ever. Biomedical research has never been
more abundant, exciting, or relevant. The result is explosive expansion
of the scientific knowledge base and technical capabilities of the pro-

fession. Medical advances are front-page news on a daily basis. Practicing medicine is becoming more efficient and prevention-oriented. Although government-designed health care reform has not materialized, market-driven reform is having a dramatic impact both on the practice of medicine and on medical education. Primary care specialization is being encouraged, while at the same time there are disincentives to specialize in other areas.

Blessed with an abundance of talented applicants, admissions committees use multiple steps in their quest to select the best medical students. For the applicant, a crucial objective is to get an interview. Various committees approach this decision point in the overall selection process differently. For example, some schools send secondary applications only to those who pass screening criteria, while others send secondary applications to all who apply and evaluate them later in other ways. Nonetheless, all committees decide whom to interview based on written application materials including grades, MCAT scores, the applicants' personal statements, and recommendations.

Year after year, applicants ask the same questions: What is the best undergraduate major? What are medical schools looking for? Should I do research? How important are extracurricular activities? How do admissions committees decide? What are the trick questions? The authors of this book offer sound advice as they address these questions and many more.

However, all applicants should prepare themselves before they sit down to fill out the applications by figuring out the answers to a few key questions: What about medicine appeals to you? How does medicine relate to your personal goals, plans, and vision of the future? What experiences have you had to indicate that you and medicine are right for each other?

After you know the answers to these questions, representing yourself on paper and telling your story in the interview are a piece of cake.

W. Edwin Dodson, M.D.

Associate Vice Chancellor and Associate
Dean for Admissions and Continuing Medical Education
Washington University School of Medicine
St. Louis, Missouri

CONTENTS

INTRODUCTION

O **NE OF THE MOST DIFFICULT THINGS** to do when applying to medical school is to decipher which advice is accurate and which is not. The main problem is that most of the people giving advice have never actually gone through the admissions process themselves. That's why this book is unique.

As recent medical students, we have firsthand knowledge of the admissions process and can give you perhaps the best and most realistic advice you'll ever hear. Often, books and counselors do more to *dis*courage the applicant than *en*courage. Well, we're not going to tell you that in order to be a doctor you have to make straight A's, climb Mount Everest, or be Ms. Wonderful-Everything, because the fact is, you don't.

We believe that getting into medical school is not an insurmountable task, and that what most doctors actually do in their daily practice does not require a genius intellect or qualify them for a Nobel Prize. Instead, we believe that the whole admissions process is a formula, a game with set rules. If you play the game by the rules, you'll get in. It's that simple. Our goal is to tell you exactly what the formula entails, as we have learned from our own experience and from

> *The best effect of*
>
> *any book is that it*
>
> *excites the reader*
>
> *to self activity.*
>
> *—Thomas Carlyle*

interviews with admissions committee members.

A major attraction in our book, we believe, is the large number of actual application essays (a.k.a. "personal statements") collected from students admitted to top medical colleges around the country. Applicants can spend months writing and perfecting their essays, and every year premedical students scramble and search for successful essays to read. We think the collection will be invaluable in showing you how broad the range of potential topics is, and it should give you an idea of what gets admissions committees excited. Plus, we hope the essays will inspire your own creativity and relieve some anxiety.

Another anxious time for the applicant to medical school is the interview. The uncertainties and fears surrounding this part of the process give students nightmares. So, we have accumulated a list of questions that interviewers have asked applicants during actual interviews. We have also researched what interviewers typically seek during an interview. Applicants rarely know how their applications and responses are evaluated, or what questions are likely to arise in the interview. These pieces of information are exactly what you need to turn what might be just good interviews into really great interviews.

We also recommend additional reading, rank the country's medical schools, provide the latest information on the MCAT, and include a timetable that allows you to track and check your progress throughout the application process. Most important, we encourage premedical students to apply with confidence, and we suggest ways they can properly market their strengths.

It may also be useful to mention what this book is not. This book will not help you decide if medicine is the right career for you. That decision can come only from working in a hospital and observing physicians. Also, we make no attempt to glorify or romanticize medicine; we'll leave that to *ER* and *Patch Adams*. Instead, we hope to convince you that half the battle in the medical school admissions game is thinking positively and knowing how to work within the system.

Once you have these insights, you'll realize that it's not necessary to be cutthroat to get into medical school. On the contrary, the best physicians are not chemistry lab nerds who would sabotage a neighbor's experiment. They are thoughtful, caring, well-rounded people with wide-ranging interests. If you would like to be this kind of physician, read on, because what follows is the ultimate set of insiders' tips for medical school admissions success!

1

P R E M E D I C A L
P R E P A R A T I O N

*B*ASICALLY, THERE ARE THREE TYPES of premedical students. The first is the most familiar. They knew they were going to be physicians from the very beginning. At age two, they were playing with stethoscopes. In high school, they chose a college based on how it would affect their medical school acceptance. The second and probably largest group are those who decided to undertake the quest for medical school in their undergraduate years. The third group consists of people who decided on med school after college graduation—and sometimes after being established in another career.

While different in many ways, all three groups share two common misconceptions. First, they think that just because medicine draws upon science, every premed should major in biology or chemistry. Second, they think the quality of their college and their major are decisive factors in their admission to medical school.

In fact, nothing could be further from the truth. Because the spectrum of physicians is so broad, there is no preferred major to enter the medical profession. In some cases, the quality of the undergraduate university can affect your chances of admission to medical school, but usually it's irrelevant. (An important exception are undergraduate colleges that have affiliated medical schools. More on this later.)

Despite worries over physicians' incomes shrinking because of health care reform measures, a recent issue of *Money Magazine* ranked "physician" as the second-best job in America, after "computer systems analyst." So it's not too surprising that many premedical student are conscious (almost paranoid) about the most minor details of their undergraduate curriculum. The unfortunate reality is that the paranoia is unfounded. It's based on pervasive myths spread by other premedical students, not on the true details that admissions committees consider important.

So what is important? At the risk of over-simplifying, you must have (or create) a quality that makes you stand out from the pack. Standing out is another way of saying that you are "interesting," and "interesting" is what medical schools go for.

Once you decide to pursue medical school, it's essential that you remain you. It's okay to explore your talents and curiosity in college; indeed, we heartily recommend it. Go ahead and learn to scuba dive or take a course on Emily Dickinson, if that's what you'd like to do. With this philosophy, you need not worry about the person next to you all the time, and you'll be much more relaxed. If you want to become a "doctor to the stars" in Hollywood, get a degree in business or, better yet, film. Don't laugh! Patients want to be able to relate to their doctors.

If you are like most premedical students, you probably don't know what kind of doctor you want to become. So our advice is simple: major in whatever interests you.

Planning Your Undergraduate Study

When medical schools receive an applicant's grades, they look at the overall grade point average, as well as the GPA derived exclusively from science courses.

Now, you non-science majors probably realize your potential disadvantage in this procedure. That is, if an English major gets a C in freshman chemistry, he'll have a pitiful science grade point average, because he won't have many science courses to average with the C. That lone C will stand as indicative of mediocre scientific ability— though it may in fact be a false represen- tation. We know all the sob stories about your bad semester that year. You had family problems, girl- or boyfriend problems, a lingering case of beriberi, etc. Unfortu- nately, while these stories are often true and relevant, medical schools give little if any consideration to such deficiencies unless you show marked improvement and

In the long run of history, the censor and the inquisitor have always lost. The only sure weapon against bad ideas is better ideas. The source of better ideas is wisdom. The surest path to wisdom is a liberal education.

—A. Whitney Griswold

progress later in your transcript.

So if you're a non-science major and you've got a poor science grade, you'll need to spend extra effort to raise your science average. If your grade is poor in a course, take the course again if you can get the bad grade erased. If you can't get it erased but merely averaged with the new grade, we don't advise taking the course over. Instead, take a more advanced science course, which will average the low grade plus look better and more purposeful on your transcript.

Medical schools today seem to have had enough of the eggheads, and they are leaning more towards people with degrees in the liberal arts and science majors who are "well-rounded." In fact, history majors have some of the highest percentages of acceptance to medical colleges, and biology majors some of the lowest, within each of their respective groups. (Of course, this doesn't mean you should switch your major to history, because an alternative interpretation of this statistic is possible: a higher percentage of mediocre applicants are biology majors, since nearly every biology major applies to medical school.)

We have a friend, a straight-A biomedical engineer, who interviewed at Washington University. One of the first things they told him was, "Frankly, Mr. Smith, we've found that English majors make the best doctors." Don't get us wrong—he had no trouble getting accepted there. The point is, it's wrong to think that you must be a science major to be a doctor, or that being a science major will give you an advantage when applying to medical school.

A premedical student must fulfill certain science requirements: one year of inorganic chemistry, one year of organic chemistry, one year of physics, and one year of biology. Other required subjects, such as English and calculus, vary with different med schools. Past these, you can study almost anything you want.

At many schools, the science courses are extremely difficult, especially at schools with a good science reputation. This is also often the case at large universities, where classes with over 700 premedical students are common. Usually, organic chemistry is the "weed-out" class. Well, here's some good news: you don't need to be part of a "weed-out," and you don't have to sit back and take it. If you can take organic elsewhere, where it's easier and maybe even cheaper, then by all means do so. An A is an A on your transcript, no matter where you got it. However, make certain your college will allow you to transfer the course credit before you spend your summer in a classroom.

All of you have heard people say that they were going to take so-and-so science course because they thought it would help them in medical school or look good to admissions committees. This is the most absurd way of assuring yourself an A or an honors later in medical school. Med schools apparently agree with us, since most discourage students from taking courses that resemble the first year's curriculum. (Genetics and biochemistry are occasional exceptions.)

The best way to get an A in med school is simply to work hard for it when the time comes. Unless you are truly interested in the sciences, you will not make your transcript look more impressive by taking med school-level courses as an undergraduate. In fact, you'll probably make it look worse, because your grade point average will be lower. Anyway, when you don't have to worry about advanced courses, you'll have more time to go to the beach or the mountains.

The hardest hurdle to jump is getting into a medical school. Therefore, any method that lets you take short cuts, have fun, and still get in is a perfectly acceptable alternative to killing yourself by studying 24 hours a day for courses that you may never use again in your life.

The rationale is simple: you'll learn everything you need to know to be a doctor during med school and your residency. You don't need to be Isaac Newton's clone, and you don't need advanced courses on the undergraduate level. You simply need to show aptitude and a minimum amount of knowledge about science so you can survive the curriculum. Completing your undergraduate degree with good grades merely tells a medical college that you have the stamina to persevere for four years and succeed. In general, it's a good indication of your ability to do well in medical school, because the coursework in med school is just like undergraduate coursework, but at much higher endurance levels.

Picking the Right Undergraduate College

Many medical schools will tell applicants from junior colleges and some state universities that, statistically, they are at a distinct disadvantage to applicants who went to a private university or a respected state school. The reason is that GPA's earned at the former are not deemed as valuable as those from more competitive schools. We agree that this is unfair, especially since many people must attend such schools for economic or geographic reasons.

So what do you do if you go to Mediocre State Tech? Pack it up and transfer? Certainly not! You'll just have to be that much better than the others, and your GPA should be that much higher.

Does this mean that med schools make numerical adjustments on GPA's depending on what college you attended? Yes, many do. Obviously, this hurts individuals high on the scale whose grades are adjusted down, since it's impossible to achieve higher than a 4.0 average. On the other hand, admissions committees often inflate the value of grades from prestigious colleges, so a lot of boneheads get in from top schools. Hey, who said life is fair?

You basically have two choices: transfer to a better school, if that's the problem, or work really hard where you are. We favor doing the latter, rather than worrying about the alma mater.

However, there is one case when we suggest you transfer. If you have the choice, always go to a university with a medical school. Twenty percent of the students at some medical schools attended that school as an undergraduate. Obviously, the university must show that it believes in its own product, so, statistically, its own premeds have a notable advantage over other applicants when they apply to their university's med school.

> *It is all one to me if a man comes from Sing Sing or Harvard. We hire a man, not his history.*
>
> *—Henry Ford*

Nevertheless, if you are good, it doesn't matter where you went to college. You'll stand out sooner or later. Besides, medical colleges have devised a way out of such subjective dilemmas—it's called the MCAT. It turns all students—whether they're from Yale or Tinyburg Tech—into an objective number. If you do well on the MCAT, you'll likely get into medical school.

So don't lose sleep about which undergraduate school you should attend. Go to the college that appeals to you because of location, price, curriculum, sports program, or other personal reasons. If chemistry and physics are your thing, then go to a school known for sciences. The same logic applies if you're interested in drama or art.

The real bottom line is how you measure up as a person. College may give you the only opportunity to enjoy and explore things that really excite you other than medicine. After all, health professionals treat people and must be personable, not simply mechanics fixing machines. They must have a well-rounded intelligence, as well as scientific knowledge, since they deal with incredible technology—and everyday patients.

So don't be one-dimensional, the stereotypical premed nerd, grinding away for hours in the library and the lab. Use your undergraduate experience creatively and explore college opportunities to their fullest. It will do wonders to shape you as a whole person, and it will make you a much better doctor someday.

Post-Baccalaureate Programs

Designed to get people into medical school after they've graduated from college, post-baccalaureate programs are especially attractive to older applicants who have decided midway through a different career to pursue medicine but lack the required premed courses. Dr. W. Edwin Dodson, Associate Vice Chancellor and Associate Dean for Admissions and Continuing Medical Education at Washington University School of Medicine in St. Louis, sees such programs springing up all over the place. As to whether they help, well, "outcome is directly related to cause," he said. Students who fall back on post-baccalaureate programs to remedy a poor undergraduate record are less likely to benefit than engineers who simply lack a few required courses.

Some programs are open only to minority or disadvantaged students, including those who have previously applied to medical school unsuccessfully. Others, designed specifically for those who are changing careers and lack course prerequisites, may require a minimum undergraduate GPA for eligibility.

Consider each program's record, too. Both the University of Pennsylvania and Columbia, for example, have high placement records. Columbia also has a specific admissions relationship with several medical schools. Other schools' records are spotty, so *caveat emptor*.

As of this writing, about 115 schools offer formal post-baccalaureate programs—too many for us to list here. For more information, call the medical schools you're interested in attending, or check out the AAMC web site (see below).

Using the Internet

There are numerous personal, commercial, and academic Web sites offering information useful to the medical school applicant. Surfing the net is also a huge time sink, so here are a few sites you may want to try before you waste large amounts of your precious free time:

AAMC (www.aamc.org)—The student and applicant information part of this site contains the AMCAS-E electronic application form (throw your typewriter away!), and information on special programs, financial aid, and the MCAT.

www.premedical.com—This site has a well-attended premed chat group, but keep in mind that you're mainly dealing with other premeds. There is also a useful survey on books and courses used to prepare for the MCAT.

Interviewfeedback.com—Browse surveys completed by applicants who have gone through the medical school interview process.

Erick's Guide to Medical School Admissions (lonestar.texas.net/ ~ santos/MedGuide.html)—One of many personal web pages with advice on how to get into medical school.

Brad's Premed Resource Center (www.geocities.com/ CollegePark/Union/8194/premed.html)—Contains a long list of links to a variety of medically related sites. Some links are outdated, but overall, it's a useful site to browse.

2

POWER TECHNIQUES
FOR HIGHER GRADES

*I*T'S COMMON KNOWLEDGE THAT GOOD GRADES are essential for gaining acceptance to medical school. The problem is, "good" is rarely defined.

For those who don't have perfect grade point averages, the belief that "the higher the GPA, the better" can cause some real mental anguish—especially if you use the class valedictorian as your standard. On the other hand, you're kidding yourself if you think medical schools admit students at the bottom of the class. Of course, reality is somewhere between these two extremes.

Here's a real life example: During our volunteer work in an urban emergency room, a physician told us he had a 2.0 average as an undergraduate majoring in chemistry. After graduation, he didn't know what he wanted to do with his life, so he went to Africa with the Peace Corps for two years. Helping a lot of suffering people there convinced him that medicine was his calling. He returned to the United States and took a year of graduate courses, after which he entered medical school.

In contrast, we know an applicant from a prestigious college who had nearly perfect grades and MCAT scores. Almost every medical school rejected him. The problem was that nothing in his record made him unique or revealed a sincere desire to study medicine.

The lesson, then, is simple: there's not always a clear grade break determining who will and who won't be accepted. In fact, some medical schools don't even have a minimum GPA requirement. For the sake of being realistic though, you should have at least a 3.0—unless your MCAT scores are quite high or you have special circumstances in your personal life.

Some of you may think such grades are difficult to attain. However, we believe a 3.0 or higher is a realistic goal for just about anybody, if you go about it correctly.

Techniques for Grade Point Success

Although you may be familiar with some of the techniques outlined in this chapter, many people do not adhere to even the most basic points. The irony is, those who don't practice good study habits are often the same students who complain about how difficult their courses are. Therefore, if you fall into this group, or even if you don't, refresh your memory about good, basic study techniques. These concepts can make your courses seem much easier.

1. Get old exams.

The first golden rule to success in college courses is to study old exams. Professors are not so creative that they can devise original exam questions each year. In fact, they often don't have time to change the test much at all. So you'll frequently see either the same or very similar questions on old exams.

Some of you may think, "I don't need old exams, because if I really know the material I'll ace the exam anyway." We thought the same thing until reality (and a few C's) hit us in the face. Many questions that involve concepts require insight from the student, and insight requires time—usually more time than allowed on exams. Exposure to similar or identical concepts days before an exam will put you way ahead of others who are seeing the problem for the first time

Using this technique, a two-letter increase in your grades is common (i.e., from a C to an A). You can get old exams from upper classmates, teaching assistants, or sometimes the professor, if you explain that most of the class has them. Hustling for old exams is a skill you should learn and constantly refine, since you'll need it later in medical school, where exams are even more repetitive and predictable.

Of course, this must all be done within the realm of honest, ethical behavior. Cheaters don't get into med school.

2. Take a reasonable course load.

Another golden rule to success in college: don't overload your class schedule. Most students realize that if they had more time, they could do better in their courses. In other words, the problem is not that certain courses are intrinsically difficult; it's that they are time-consuming, and they take time away from all your other courses.

Don't get the wrong idea—we are not suggesting that you attend school part-time. Rather, we suggest you eliminate super-macho schedules. For example, some students think they can take four laboratory courses in one semester and still get a 3.7 GPA. If you can, more power to you, and we'll congratulate you when you get the Nobel Prize. However, most students get only poor grades and lots of stress.

A reasonable schedule means more time. More time means less stress. Less stress means you will enjoy the courses you're taking and think more deeply about them. It's ironic that, although a university exists to foster creative thinking, most students feel such time pressure that creative thought becomes nearly impossible.

3. Study alone.
For most circumstances, we advise you to study alone.

Many people insist that group study is best because you're forced to think hard about the topic when you must explain it to someone else. As a result, they say, group study will expose weaknesses in your comprehension.

It sounds good, but most group study doesn't work out that way. Instead of quizzing each other and discussing topics relevant to the course, you spend a lot of your time gossiping about the party last weekend. If your study partner is attractive, you won't be concentrating on the material. Plus, there's usually somebody in the group who only wants to be tutored, and he's so far behind that he can't contribute anything. (He's usually the same person who asks you for lecture notes because he felt class wasn't as important as his sleep.)

Don't misunderstand—sometimes it is appropriate to form a group to tackle class material. If a professor is disorganized and confusing, a study session with good students can clear up tough concepts. And topics that require a lot of memorization are easier to learn if another person quizzes you (e.g., organic chemistry reactions).

But nine times out of ten, you're better off studying alone, without all the distractions of a group.

4. Choose the proper study environment.
Study in a quiet place that's not too comfortable. Some people claim they can study on a couch while they watch MTV. For most students, however, this is the first step to disaster. Courses like physics and

chemistry require deep, sustained concentration, and distractions like TV and radio only hinder good studying. College life comes with many freedoms that can make grades suffer if a student can't impose self-discipline. Part of being a physician (or an adult, for that matter) is knowing when to work and when to play. Developing such habits early will make life much easier in the future.

A library-like environment is where you will study most efficiently. If you study on your bed, odds are you'll fall asleep. Unfortunately, many libraries are uncomfortable. You should find a quiet, comfortable place where you can think intensely for long hours.

5. Highlight your books.

Students from most public high schools, where it is a capital offense to put even a light pencil mark in a textbook, may have a tough time with this. However, universities require students to purchase their own books, and usually at high prices. Since you own these expensive texts, it's totally acceptable and certainly advisable to write in them.

Highlighting is a good way to filter out minor details, and it's an excellent way to review for exams. If you don't write in your texts because you want to keep them in pristine condition, you're making studying much more difficult than it need be. Besides, the resale value of marked-up books is exactly the same as clean books.

6. Make flash cards.

Most people do not like to use flash cards because it reminds them of learning multiplication tables in third grade. But flash cards are the most useful—and least used—study technique.

Flash cards appear to be expensive and time-consuming to make. This is true only if you wait until the end of a course to make them. We have found that folding a regular sheet of paper into sixteen squares and then cutting them out makes the best size (and least expensive) flash cards. Use paper clips to keep them in convenient bundles, and make them as you go along with your studies.

For instance, when you highlight a concept in a book, write it on a flash card as a question, with the question on one side and the answer on the other. Once you've made the cards, even material that involves simple regurgitation will be easier to learn. Since you already wrote them, the cards make reviewing the material as fast and as good as, if not better than, being quizzed by another student.

7. Maintain a social life.

Although many college students tend to socialize at the expense of good grades, some premeds go to the opposite extreme and withdraw entirely from the fun of college life. But that's a mistake, because social relaxation provides an excellent release for tension and prevents burnout. Moreover, a moderate social life will actually enhance your academics. You'll find that wasting an evening at the movies or at the local tavern will put you in a much better mood to study organic chemistry the next morning.

A social life will keep your eyes open to the rest of the world and will remind you that there's more to life than the basement of the library. Your undergraduate years should be some of the best years of your life, so it only makes sense to enjoy them as much as possible.

8. Understand concepts that seem unlikely to appear on the exam.

Professors realize there are certain topics with which most students have problems. Many times we would say to ourselves, "He'd never test us on this stuff. It's too hard, and he spent only five minutes discussing it." Guess what? The obscure stuff would always be on the exam, and they were always the questions that most of the class got wrong.

Most professors write exams with a bell curve in mind: there are questions everyone should be able to answer, questions some people should be able to answer, and a few questions that only the top students will get. Topics that seem trivial and ambiguous are, as one professor told us, "excellent material with which to separate the A students from the B students."

Look at it this way: it's just a game, so be a smart player and pay attention to even the most minor details.

9. Don't memorize when you can understand.

If you can learn something by either memorizing it or conceptually understanding it, always choose the latter. Generally, it's less efficient to memorize many details than to understand a general principle from which you can derive the specifics.

Learning things this way will help you excel in courses like physics and chemistry, where exam questions are not identical to, but similar to, the homework problems. If you understand the principle well, you'll be able to apply the concept to the problem on the exam.

Improving Grades by Being Assertive

Although studying hard is probably the single most important factor in achieving high grades, there are times when being aggressive may be just what it takes to push you from a B+ to an A-.

Unfortunately, some students take this philosophy to the extreme, and it only works against them. They are perceived as obnoxious, and teaching assistants and students avoid helping them. Some of these "grade grubbers" will argue for every little point on every exam. When it comes time for recommendations, you can bet professors tell medical schools about a grade grubber's real personality.

On the other hand, letting professors or T.A.'s get away with grading errors or unfairness is no good either. So, you should try to walk that fine line between being an overaggressive jerk and being a piece of driftwood. By doing this, you can sometimes push your grade a little higher.

For example, don't be afraid during a lecture to ask the professor to explain a concept again. Better yet, ask the professor about it after class. It may turn up on the exam, and professors instinctively try to help students with material related to exam questions. When the student gets the question right, the professor feels he has done an excellent job teaching the material!

Also, get to know your teaching assistant. You don't have to be a brown-noser, but you should ask for help whenever you need it. If the T.A. sees that you're making a sincere effort, he'll be more willing to help you and may even boost your grade if you're on a borderline.

Finally, stand up for your rights. Tell your professors and/or T.A.'s if you think they are out of line (e.g., giving what you think is a bad test, not spending enough time on a difficult concept, etc.). Don't threaten and don't whine, but talk to them in a rational, mature manner. You'll be surprised how interested they are in your opinion. They'll usually make changes or suggest ways you can overcome your difficulty.

Pass/Fail Grades

An easy and enjoyable way to take a course is on a pass/fail basis. Unfortunately, competition for medical school makes taking your required premedical courses pass/fail unadvisable, because med schools have no way to interpret what a "pass" means in relation to your peers. Taking a few courses like sailing or drama pass/fail isn't a problem, but never take Organic pass/fail!

If you attend a college that uses a pass/fail system in lieu of all grades, request that your work be graded. It is unfortunate that stimulating learning experiences must be perverted into a scramble for grades, but that's the premedical reality.

3

T H E M C A T

W **E CANNOT OVEREMPHASIZE** the importance of good MCAT scores in the medical school admissions game. Though standardized tests continue to be criticized as culturally biased and dehumanizing, the MCAT remains the standard by which medical schools level grades from many different colleges.

Nearly all medical schools require the MCAT. It's crucial that your scores be as high as possible, because at many med schools, only the combination of your grades and your MCAT scores determines whether you get an interview letter or a rejection letter. If you're attending an expensive Ivy League school, you may slide by with slightly lower MCAT scores, but for the most part it's a very cold, objective process.

The moral of the story is simple: Don't treat lightly something that may mean as much as—if not more than—three years of grades combined.

MCAT Sections

The current MCAT consists of four sections, including a writing sample. The test lasts five hours and 45 minutes, but when you add a lunch break and the usual standardized testing delays, you'll be there seven or eight hours.

Section One of the exam, called **Verbal Reasoning** (a.k.a. "reading comprehension"), involves multiple-choice questions drawn from passages about 500 words long. The topics are selected at random from the humanities, social sciences, and natural sciences, and you aren't expected to have any prior knowledge of the subjects.

People who usually do well on reading comprehension tests should have no trouble on this section. English majors, for example, will have a real advantage, since they have typically done more critical reading than the average science major. If you're anxious about this section, there's really only one solution: read more! One recent test-taker suggested reading newspaper editorials, since their length and style approximate the Verbal Reasoning passages fairly well. But in the long run, you'll probably help yourself just as much by getting a good night's sleep and eating a light breakfast before the exam.

Section Two, **Physical Sciences**, consists of physics and chemistry questions. You're expected to answer the questions based on your knowledge of basic science concepts, plus your comprehension of the information presented in passages, graphs, and tables that accompany the questions. Unlike Section One, you can greatly improve your score in Section Two through intensive review of course material.

After lunch, you get Section Three, the **Writing Sample**, which requires you to write two essays, each based on a quotation or statement. You have 30 minutes for each essay. This section has been evolving since its introduction several years ago. The instructions for each essay used to be identical, but now they vary with the topic. The AAMC has made a (long) list of topics available on its web site (www.aamc.org), and the actual questions for the 1999 MCAT's were taken from this list. Needless to say, the list is worth a look. The key to this section is to remember that the graders are expecting only a "first draft" effort. Don't get caught with an unfinished essay because you've been rewriting, revising, and polishing your interpretation. It's far more important to complete the essays in an organized, coherent—if rough—fashion.

Section Three is made more challenging by the fact that it begins right after lunch. Often, people finish Section Two feeling very hungry, so they gorge themselves at lunch. Then they return to the testing room and start to feel drowsy, suffering from what we call "food coma." When the time comes to write the second essay, their minds have turned to mush.The remedy for this is easy: don't eat large portions of red meat or greasy food at lunch. Instead, eat trail mix, salad, fish, chicken, or other light fare. If you don't stuff yourself during lunch and remain calm while writing, you shouldn't have overwhelming problems with Section Three.

Section Four, **Biological Sciences**, is identical in format to Section Two, but there are two big differences. First, the questions address biology and organic chemistry. Second, it's the last section of the test, and you'll undoubtedly be sick and tired of filling in those little bubbles with your #2 pencil.

The solution to the first problem is simple: study. The solution to the fatigue is a little sneakier. Bring something sugary, like a Snickers bar, in your pocket. Technically, food is not allowed in the testing room, but most monitors won't make a big deal about it as long as you're not bothering anyone. (By the way, we were strongly rebuked in an *Academic Medicine* review of our book for even suggesting that you do something sneaky at the MCAT's.) During Section Three, eat the candy. If you time it right, you should have a big sugar high to get you through the last section. So after the test you lapse into a food coma. But who cares? It's over!

It's important to remember that the MCAT is designed to break you and everyone else. The propaganda written by the test-makers will tell you that the MCAT will measure the "problem-solving" and "communication" skills necessary for your career as a physician. Maybe. What it really measures is your endurance, which is probably the most important quality you need to be a doctor anyway.

With the MCAT you have no choice: you must play their game, by their rules. But you can play it smart. Everyone knows it's just a weeder, so don't get hyper-anxious and let yourself become a weed that gets plucked.

Scoring the MCAT

The MCAT gives four scores, which reflect your performance in each section. The scores for Verbal Reasoning, Physical Sciences, and Biological Sciences are reported on a scale of 1-15 (with 15 as the highest). Your raw score—the actual number of correctly answered problems—is converted to this 1-15 scale so people who take different MCAT's can be compared to one another.

In the Writing Sample, two readers grade each essay "holistically," which can be best defined as "by gut feeling." You don't get one point for spelling, one point for sentence structure, one point for grammar, and so on. Instead, readers give a single score for their overall impression of the essay. However, your score will be reduced automatically if you don't address all three tasks required in each essay. The four essay scores (two per essay) are combined into one raw score, which gets converted to an alphabetical scale of J to T (with T as the highest).

Although your raw score may be lower than the raw score of

someone who took the MCAT after you, your scaled score may be the same, because it reflects your performance among your peers who took the test at the same time—and that's the truly useful data. The test makers do their best to offer equivalent MCAT's from year to year. They adjust for the slight variations in each test-taking population by shifting the bell curve that corresponds to the scaled scores.

Many med schools look for consistency in MCAT scores. If your three numerical scores are above 10 and your essay score is respectable, your chances of an interview are quite good. But two 14's on the science sections won't help if you got a 6 in Verbal Reasoning and your essay score is appropriate for someone who drew pretty pictures on the paper. And while many programs will state that they use the writing sample score as part of their evaluation of an applicant, a much smaller percentage actually bother to read the essays themselves.

Interestingly, studies have found only moderate correlation between high MCAT scores and good medical school performance during the first two years. There is no correlation at all with clinical clerkship grades. Nonetheless, medical schools will continue to use the MCAT to make decisions about applicants, so you're just going to have to deal with it.

Preparing for the MCAT

When you receive your MCAT registration packet from the Association of American Medical Colleges, you'll read on the second page of the instruction booklet something like, "The AAMC has conducted analyses comparing the performances of examinees who enroll in commercial review courses with those who do not (*yak, yak, yak, blah, blah, blah*), and we have found that gains derived from taking commercial review courses are small—only one-half of one scaled score point."

Now, this may sound like doing well on the MCAT has something to do with genetics or your intrinsic intelligence or something crazy like that. Well, that's simply bunk! The MCAT is not the SAT, and it's not about seeing three dimensional relationships in space, *a la* IQ tests. It's about knowing old concepts so well that they're as fresh as when you first learned them two or three years ago.

The point is, there are no curve balls on the MCAT, and studying for it, as for any other test, will boost your scores.

But there are no short cuts, either. Preparing for the MCAT requires a lot of diligence—and diligence is what the MCAT measures! Getting high scores is really a function of how badly you want to get in, and, in our opinion, how badly you want to get in is the most important information an admissions committee can have about your potential success.

The earlier you start preparing, the better. Reviewing for the MCAT will involve effort as any other test—just much, much more. We recommend you start the review at least six (and probably nine) months before the exam. This doesn't mean reading an MCAT review book five minutes before you go to bed. You should start an intensive review of concepts and information that will be pertinent to the exam (see outline in *The MCAT Student Manual*).

We cannot stress enough the importance of focusing your study on relevant topics during this critical period. For example, don't start reviewing old notes from chemistry class, because you'll only get bogged down in an incredible amount of superfluous material. You'll end up studying information in a depth that you'll never see on the MCAT. (By the way, this skill of discriminating study will be essential in medical school, where you must decide what's important from a mind-boggling amount of information.)

Remember, the MCAT tests very basic concepts. Occasionally they are disguised in a complicated question, but usually they are given in a straightforward manner.

The problem is, there are many questions on a wide range of topics, so you may be asking, "Well, how do I know which basic concepts to study and which to ignore?" Fortunately, someone has answered that question for you. Perhaps the most important investment you can make to get into medical school—besides this book, of course—is a good MCAT review book (and maybe your lucky charm of choice). In previous editions of our book, we have always recommended *The Princeton Review: Flowers & Silver MCAT*. The authors offer succinct review notes that parallel the outline of science topics in *The MCAT Student Manual*, which is written by the same people who devise the MCAT.

Get the idea? The authors imply that if you know their book thoroughly, you should average a minimum of 11 on the science portions of the MCAT. Based on our personal experiences, this is remarkably accurate.

Unfortunately, we have heard reports of numerous errors in recent editions of Flowers' and Silver's book, so we can't recommend it as highly as we once did. Another popular review book is *The Betz Guide: A Complete Preparation for the MCAT*. Interestingly, Flowers used to publish under the Betz name.

It's more difficult to increase your scores in the reading and writing sections, because they involve skills that you either have or have not developed in the course of your entire education. So don't sweat it! You can't worry about things you can't improve. Concentrate on what you most certainly can improve: your science scores.

Professional MCAT Prep Courses

What about professional preparatory courses like Stanley Kaplan and The Princeton Review? We recommend them, but you should realize that you'll get out of them only what you put into them.

Stanley Kaplan Testing Centers offer the most popular courses. Now, we all know Stan makes big bucks every year off a lot of premeds, but for about $1,000 he can do a lot more for your MCAT scores than $80,000 worth of private college will. Plus, his fee doesn't seem so large when you consider that you might spend $5,000 just *applying* to medical schools.

For most students, the in-class part of the Kaplan course is not worthwhile—they don't tell you anything you can't get on your own. What you're really buying are hundreds of simulated MCAT exams. Stan can go a little overboard with the depth of his exam questions, so if you're getting about 75% or 80% on his exams, you'll probably get 11's and 12's on the real MCAT.

We suggest you take all the Kaplan tests. Then, listen only to the recorded answers of the questions you got wrong. Finally, review the subject areas that gave you difficulty in the practice tests. This process alone will take three months to do thoroughly. We won't guarantee you'll see identical questions on the real MCAT, but you'll have solved so many similar problems that it will be a real challenge for the test-maker to write a question that doesn't resemble a problem you've already seen on a Kaplan test.

In any event, Kaplan's tests show you where you are weak, and they decrease your anxiety about the MCAT—probably their most valuable function, in the long run.

Again, to get your money's worth from any prep course, take all the sample tests and review your preparatory booklets on a regular basis. Set aside a regular time each week for intensive preparation. If you do these things consistently about 20 hours a week and begin six to nine months before the exam, almost nothing can stop you from getting good MCAT scores.

As for the authors' personal experiences: John studied Kaplan, became a believer and then an instructor. Dan also took the Kaplan course and did OK on the MCAT. Stephanie, on the other hand, regularly worked through Flowers' book, aced her MCAT's, and saved some money. Decide on the approach you think will work for you.

Examination Tips

Though some of the following suggestions may seem obvious, students often forget them during the pressure of an exam. Therefore, read through them before you take the MCAT to remind yourself of test-taking strategies, and remember to adhere to them even when the test is not going smoothly:

1. Read all directions with great care. It's ridiculous how many errors occur due to carelessness in reading directions and headings.

2. Time is a limiting factor. Remember this when you're tempted to leave a question unanswered, expecting to return to it later. The best thing to do is mark your best guess for the moment and star the question so you can go back to it later if you have time.

3. Be conscious of your allotted time. You must budget your time for each of the sections on the exam, so take a watch to the test. According to *The MCAT Student Manual*, your total score is a reflection of your right answers only. This means you aren't penalized for guessing, so always guess! Never leave any bubbles blank. If you have 30 seconds left and 10 unanswered questions, just fill in the same letter for all of them.

4. In the Verbal Reasoning section, quickly read the questions *before* you read the passage. This way, you'll recognize the sections in the passage that deal with the questions. Also, the questions are usually in the same order as the information in the passage. (Sometimes there's an early question that you can't answer until you finish the passage.) Knowing this, you can usually keep the next question in mind, read the passage until you come to the answer, and then move on. By doing this, you read the passage only once and save a lot of time.

5. Do not use your own knowledge in the Verbal Reasoning section to answer any questions. All questions are based only on information in the passage. Base your answers solely on the information in the passage.

6. Before starting each essay, write a brief outline in the margin of the booklet. If you start to get bogged down in the essay, refer to the outline and recall the key points you want to express. If you try to organize it all in your head, you probably won't write a clear essay.

7. While working the science sections, rely on your fundamental understanding of chemistry, biology, and physics. Most questions in the science sections deal exclusively with basic principles.

Suggested Reading

Medical School Admission Requirements. *Association of American Medical Colleges, Att: Publications, 2450 N St. NW, Washington, DC 20037-1134. Phone 202-828-0416; fax 202-828-1123. $20.* The bible for premeds. New edition available each April.

The MCAT Student Manual (includes *MCAT Practice Test I*). *Same address as above. $20.* Do not take the MCAT without this one! It contains an authentic sample MCAT, which will give you an excellent idea of what the test is like and the kind of scores you'll receive. Similar publications are also available and can be enormously helpful: **MCAT Practice Test II and Sample Items**, **MCAT Practice Test III**, and newly available **Test IV** (actual MCAT's administered a few years ago). **Practice Tests II** and **III** are $20 each; **Practice Test IV** is $35. For those who wish to save a little money, sets are available. For example, it costs $85 to order all of the above as a package.

Minority Student Opportunities in United States Medical Schools. *Also at AAMC address above. $12.* Many special programs are available to minority students, and this is the official directory.

THE APPLICATION
PROCESS

I N THE PRECEDING CHAPTERS, we described ways you can achieve your highest potential grade point average and MCAT score. After you've followed these recommendations, the time will finally come for you to apply to medical schools and show admissions committees why you should be allowed to enter their schools. It is the most critical and, in some ways, the most difficult step.

You'll probably feel frustrated when you realize that you're expected to transfer years of preparation and effort onto four pieces of paper. While we agree this may not be the best way to evaluate an applicant, we are not writing a critique of the admissions process here. We just want to tell you how to work best within the system and how to make the system work for you. As far as admissions committees are concerned, you are only what your application says you are (until the interview), and you should use this fact to your advantage.

If admissions committees were able to live with applicants and see them as they really are, they'd probably reject most of them. So here's a flaw in the process that works for you: those four sheets of paper are not very good at revealing what a person is really like. With a little effort, anyone can shine on

> *The closest to*
>
> *perfection a person*
>
> *ever comes is when*
>
> *he fills out a job*
>
> *application form.*
>
> *—Stanley J. Randall*

an application. Often, applicants are unsuccessful simply because they haven't mastered the ability to manipulate the process to their advantage as well as others. Our goal is to refine your skills of manipulation.

The two components of your application that are already set in stone are your GPA and MCAT scores. You can't change them, so don't worry about them. Your "personal statement" (usually a biographical essay) and recommendations are items you'll complete shortly before you send your application. (The end of this chapter has a timetable of events in the application process. Use it to mark your progress and keep track of important dates.)

If you already have good grades, don't write anything in your essay that could give a bad impression (e.g., extremist political views, embarrassing personal details, etc.). If your grades aren't so great, the essay is your chance to show what you're really made of. An excellent essay and glowing recommendations are the only items in the application over which you have control. Their careful execution is critical, and we will discuss them in greater detail shortly.

Remember, your application is the only "you" that medical schools will know. If they are impressed with the "you" on the application, they will want to see the real you for an interview.

AMCAS and the Application

Years ago, applying to medical school was an even more laborious task. Students had to fill out a separate application for every school—a time-consuming process, as you can imagine.

Fortunately, the American Medical College Application Service (AMCAS) has simplified the process. You can now send one application to AMCAS, which will forward copies to the schools you specify. There's even an electronic version of the application that lets you file by computer. Unfortunately, a few medical colleges are still not part of AMCAS, and you must request separate applications from each of these schools. At this writing, non-AMCAS schools are:

- **Baylor**
- **Brown**
- **Columbia**
- **Johns Hopkins**
- **New York University**
- **Texas Tech**

- **U. Missouri, Kansas City**
- **U. North Dakota**
- **U. Texas (Southwestern, San Antonio, Galveston, Houston)**
- **Yale**

You'll find these schools' addresses at the end of this book and in *Medical School Admission Requirements* (see previous chapter), which should be your bible. It includes every essential piece of information on admission statistics and requirements you could possibly imagine. Get it. You'll refer to it often.

AMCAS is just the first level of the application process. When you make it through AMCAS, you'll get a secondary application unique for each school. They range from a more detailed version of the AMCAS application to a simple request for more money "so we may further evaluate your application."

After the secondary application, you'll be asked for an interview. Rejection can come at any stage, but making it through AMCAS is the most important hurdle, because after it the process gets a little more personal and subjective. It's easier to be "creative" post-AMCAS than in the pre-AMCAS, GPA-and-MCAT-only stage.

You can get an AMCAS application from your advisor, from AMCAS medical schools, or from AMCAS directly at

> **AMCAS**
> **Section for Student Services**
> **2501 M Street, NW; Lbby-26**
> **Washington, DC 20037-1300**
> **(phone 202-828-0600; e-mail amcas@aamc.org)**

Your application must include a check, which is AMCAS's fee for its distribution service. The amount depends on the number of schools to which you want your application sent. (In the most recent application process, the fee was $200 for five schools, and $25 for each school thereafter.) Then, the schools will request about $50 more when you get their secondary applications. You can get some of these fees waived if you can demonstrate financial hardship.

You must also send an official transcript to AMCAS of all college work completed. You should request this from your school early, since many large colleges are slow to respond, and the delay will hold up the rest of your AMCAS application. Most medical schools ask you to put your last semester's grades on the back of their secondary applications, saying they "won't get your latest transcripts in time." Actually, it's a sly way to test your integrity. Any discrepancy between the grades you report and official records will prompt the admissions committee to reject your application immediately.

You won't need to send your MCAT scores to the medical schools, since AMCAS is the same swell bunch that gave you the MCAT. How convenient....

Both the AMCAS application and the secondary applications have deadlines. A golden rule in this game is to submit every application at the earliest allowed date. Many people think medical schools wait for all applications, make their selections, and reject the rest. Nothing could be further from the truth. Students are accepted on a rolling basis. In other words, for every day after the earliest possible date you wait to send your application, you have less and less chance of being admitted. Many qualified applicants have been shocked into reality when they waited until the last minute to apply and found that no spaces remained.

Your Extracurricular Activities

Extracurricular activities are very important to your application—never believe otherwise—because they tell medical schools things about you that your GPA and MCAT's never will. Of course, med schools first want to know that you're intellectually competent, but they also want to see more than just scores and a high IQ. Extracurricular activities demonstrate your personality, your motivation level, and even your basis for choosing medicine.

A man may be so much of everything that he is nothing of anything.

—Samuel Johnson

Before you say, "I want to be a doctor," it's crucial to know why you really mean it. Spending all your time making an A in Organic Chemistry will never tell you if medicine is your calling. Therefore, it's imperative that you go to a hospital and do some sort of medical work. If a hospital won't employ you, volunteer. You'll gain experience and knowledge, and you'll show medical schools that you're genuinely motivated and interested. When they ask, "So, Mr. Smith, why do you want to become a doctor?" you can say, "Well, for the past three years I've worked in an emergency room near campus, and I've found it rewarding and fascinating."

Similarly, if medical research is your thing, you can apply for summer work in a genetic engineering company or any firm engaged in biomedical research.

This way, you'll show that you've based your decision to enter medicine on practical, personal experience—experience that will convince admissions committees of the validity and conviction of your statement. (Note: Most committees actually assign points to applicants' files based on the breadth and depth of their medical-related work.)

The key concept is simple: get medical experience as an undergraduate, and make it your principal extracurricular activity. If you have an interest in a particular field of medicine, try to get work in that field. You might be surprised to learn that pediatrics, for example, isn't right for you after all. It's much better to find out early than ten years down the road, when it will be much harder to change professions.

If you don't have an interest in any specialty, don't be afraid to try anything in a hospital that will give you good experience. It may work out great, or it may bore you to tears. What's important is that it's a learning experience and a chance for you to check out the business, so to speak. Don't fool yourself by thinking that after you get accepted to medical school you'll have lots of time to decide what kind of doctor you want to be. You won't. So it's a good idea to start looking around in your college years, when making an incorrect choice won't hurt much.

If you can't find a position in a medical field that interests you, check a service-related field. For example, drug counselor, resident advisor, suicide-prevention hotline volunteer, etc. are good options. Such activities indicate your desire to help people—a very important trait. Many applicants will talk about how much they want to "help humanity," yet their only extracurriculars are "fraternity social chairman" and "captain of co-ed water polo team." No wonder admissions committees treat them with skepticism.

Finally, extracurricular work totally unrelated to medicine may be fine also. After seeing 300 applicants, interviewers tend to view everyone as pretty similar. So if you do something that interests and intrigues your interviewers, you will stick out in their minds.

For instance, if an applicant had average grades and MCAT scores and no relevant medical work—but she had won an Olympic medal— she'd probably land in medical school easily. Similarly, a college student who started his own pizza parlor or had a book published would also stand out from the pack. This doesn't mean you have to become an Olympic athlete or an entrepreneur. But if you want to do some kind of unique work, by all means do it. The main point: be interesting.

However, extracurricular activities should never come at the expense of your GPA. No amount of extracurriculars will be an excuse for poor grades. Also, it's not necessary for you to list thousands of extracurriculars on your application. A few impressive activities in which you are genuinely involved count more than a deluge of "So what?" activities.

By now, most of you probably are wondering what you can do this year to put on your application. Well, you literally can do hundreds of things. All schools have clubs. (But don't think that just because there's a premedical club you should join it. Medical schools are rarely impressed with them.) Join a club that applies to your major. Becoming a club officer always looks impressive because it shows leadership potential—an important quality for many physicians. Being an athlete is also great. Anyone who can maintain a schedule of rigorous practice and study and still keep good grades deserves to be commended. A student government office is good for similar reasons. Community volunteer work always looks good. Help out at a soup kitchen or with a literacy program, or join Big Brothers/Big Sisters.

If your school does any research at all, you should be able, with a little effort, to start working with a professor in his lab. If you are really lucky and dedicated, you may even get your name on a publication. This is extremely impressive! You might even consider being a teaching assistant in a course.

As for summer work, many universities and their medical schools sponsor programs designed especially for the undergraduate who wants hands-on experience. It's no secret that many people are admitted to medical schools through "back doors" like these. The programs offer a great opportunity for you to work for, and get to know, someone on the school's admissions committee. It doesn't guarantee you'll get in, of course, but a personal contact can't hurt. Medical schools will send you the relevant information on these programs, which often provide a stipend.

Finally, if all you can do in the summer is work in a regular job (waitress, delivery man, working for your dad, etc.) because you need the money, then that's what you must do. Just be sure to make your reasons clear in your application.

Recommendations

Letters of evaluation are one of the most important factors in the selection of medical students. Therefore, like the MCAT, you must not take them lightly.

Many applicants don't start thinking about recommendations until junior year, when they're due. Ideally, though, you should start to think about them from Day One of freshman year! Students also mistakenly assume that the person who writes your recommendation is going to write a good one. Instead, you must constantly think, "Do my professors really know me, or am I just another body in the classroom?" When the time comes to ask your professors for recommendations and they don't even know your name, you'll be in deep trouble.

> *I don't care what is written about me, so long as it isn't true.*
>
> —*Katharine Hepburn*

We all know the students constantly blathering in class—and everyone wishes they would just shut up. Well, those are people the professor remembers, too, so try to be like them—but don't be pushy and obnoxious to the point that you're remembered in a negative way. Simply be inquisitive and sound interested. Try to see your professors during their office hours and ask only a few questions to clarify major points in class. You may be surprised to find that the subject matter becomes more interesting when you force yourself to look at the material hard enough to ask intelligent questions. If your questions are intricate, save them until after the lecture. Your professor will be impressed by the depth of your understanding and appreciate your not interrupting the flow of the lecture.

Ask only "clarification" questions in class. Don't publicly correct the professor when he is wrong, but don't hesitate to do so later in the form of a question. He'll announce the correction in the next class and remember your brilliance in his recommendation letter.

A good recommendation should reflect more than just a casual acquaintance. It should also carry some weight—the more the better. You don't need to solicit Nobel laureates, but a little strategic thinking about whom you will ask can do wonders to enhance your appeal to medical schools.

A professor should be able to say more about you than, "She received a grade of A in my class." Therefore, when you ask a professor for a recommendation, ask first if he thinks he can write you a good one. Tell him to be totally honest. It's the only way to get an idea of what he'll write, since you should always request to have a closed file. (A "closed file" means you are not allowed to look at what was written about you. It's the only way to get honest, credible letters, since a professor is likely to be less candid if he knows you can read what he wrote later. This goes for both praise and criticism.)

Further, to give the admissions committee a more balanced profile, choose professors from different fields (i.e., don't get recommendations from only your chemistry professor buddies).

A recommendation from the professor with whom you do research is great because it might tell an admissions committee about your lab expertise and how well you work with others. A letter from the physician who oversees your volunteer work is also valuable, because it might describe how you deal with sick people. Sometimes, it's even a good idea to have a teaching assistant who knows you well write the recommendation, and then have the professor co-sign it (only the prof's signature gives the letter any weight).

Letters of recommendation from family, friends, medical students, and high school teachers are not acceptable. They only indicate poor judgment by the applicant.

In the past, it was common to ask a professor directly for a recommendation to send to medical schools. Today, that practice has been supplanted by a composite recommendation, where a premedical committee at your college drafts a letter of recommendation from letters written by people of your choice. This means that getting to know your premedical advisor is a very good idea. This also means that if the premedical committee can't write a good letter, it doesn't matter how good the rest of your letters were.

You can't do much about the composite letter, so don't worry about it. If the committee can't write well, your only consolation is that everybody else in your school is in the same boat. However, most composite letters include direct quotes from the professors' letters. The composite letter also ranks you in comparison to your peers in motivation, integrity, sincerity, and leadership. In addition, the letter usually begins by saying how "competitive this undergraduate institution is, and how hard it is to get good grades at this great school, etc."

Because it's all so subjective, most admissions committees ignore the bull and go straight to the quotes. Therefore, you should strongly suggest that your premedical committee include such quotes—and even the actual letters from your recommenders.

In short, the composite method has pitfalls, but try to use it to your advantage, and never make an enemy. You never know who will serve on the premedical committee.

Filling Out the Application

Since the application is your chance to tell medical schools why you are so special, give it a lot of extra care.

The first rule: it must be neat. Some students actually pay to have their essay professionally typeset, but that's probably going overboard. A good laser printer will suffice. Dr. W. Edwin Dodson at Washington University School of Medicine advises that, since members of admissions committees "tend to be old and have presbyopia, a font size less than 12 points irritates the reader"—something you definitely don't want to do.

Rule #2: the application should be totally perfect. A simple typographical error may be reason enough to reject someone when there are thousands of applicants to weed out.

Finally, don't even consider having someone else write your essay, let alone paying for such a service. Such "professional" essays are always too good to be true and will certainly raise some eyebrows. They may get you some interviews, but if your verbal skills resemble a punch-drunk boxer rather than William F. Buckley, you'll be out. Anyway, after four years of sweat, is that really the way you want to get into medical school?

> *An autobiography usually reveals nothing bad about the writer except his memory.*
>
> *—Franklin P. Jones*

Don't forget all the jobs you've held in the past few years. Many applicants never include some jobs because they think only work related to health care is significant. But any job shows a willingness to work—a trait you'll need in abundance in medical school. Besides, leaving out miscellaneous work experiences may result in that section of the application looking very empty.

Further, you never know what the person who reads your application is looking for, so include all your jobs. A member of an admissions committee told us a story that illustrates this point: An applicant's essay made the student sound so arrogant that the admissions officer was just about to toss the whole thing. Then he noticed that the student had worked a summer in construction. He wondered how someone so pretentious could do that kind of job. Intrigued, he decided to interview him. It turned out the student wasn't at all the way he sounded in his essay, and he was admitted.

You should also include all the honors you've received. Many people initially think they have no honors, but when they think harder they realize they have a few awards to write in. Remember, never leave a section blank.

You're supposed to tell your life story on the application. In other words, you're describing how you spend your time. If you spend time climbing mountains, playing the flute, designing web sites, singing opera, skydiving, organizing charity events, or anything that's just plain out of the ordinary, let them know. Medical schools always like to say how interesting and diverse their students are. They just love it if you do something eccentric or unique—and you probably do if you think about it for a while.

How Many Schools Should You Apply To?

Applying to medical school can be very expensive. You must pay for the AMCAS application, the secondary applications, and then transportation and accommodations when you interview. But compared to the cost of a medical education, the application expense is trivial. Never let money limit the number of schools to which you apply.

If you can demonstrate financial hardship, you can get the AMCAS (and sometimes the secondary application) fees waived. However, very few students are in the extremely low family income level that's required for a waiver. Often, medical schools will help reduce your expenses by letting you stay with a student when you interview.

But even after cutting lots of corners, you're still looking at a cost of $1,000-$5,000, depending on how many schools you apply to. That may sound outrageous, but consider what

There are three kinds of lies: lies, damned lies, and statistics.

—Benjamin Disraeli

your undergraduate education cost ($30,000-$100,000), then add the potential cost of medical school—another $60,000-$120,000 for tuition alone. Compared to this, even a large application budget is relatively insignificant.

Therefore, it doesn't matter whether you must beg or borrow—you should never let financial matters become a limiting factor in your application to medical school. Years of expensive work and planning should not go down the drain for a few hundred bucks.

So the question becomes, "How many schools should I apply to?" There's no easy answer, but consider the following: The average medical school receives about 5,000 applications for 100 positions. If the selection process were entirely random, your chance of acceptance would be one-in-50 (2%). To put it in a more depressing way, your chance of rejection would be 98%. Sounds pretty dismal, doesn't it?

But wait. If you apply to a number of schools, your chance of being accepted by at least one school is one minus your chance of being rejected by all of the schools. That is,

$$\% \text{ ACCEPTANCE } = 1\text{-}(.98)\text{N x } 100$$

where N is the number of schools to which you apply. Let's plug in some sample numbers:

N =	% ACCEPTANCE
1	2
5	10
10	18
20	33
30	45

In reality, of course, the process is not totally random, though there are random elements in it. The point is, even if you're a straight-A student, it would be unwise to apply to fewer than five schools. Basically, the more the better. If you are a really strong student, you should apply to no fewer than ten. If you're like most people, 20 and even 30 schools would be a good idea.

Many applicants don't realize that applying to as many medical schools as possible is as important as doing well in biology or on the MCAT. Of course, you must never compromise quality for quantity of applications.

The 2% probability of acceptance at a particular medical school is not really as bad as it sounds. In a recent entering class, 41,004 people applied for 16,170 places. So, your actual overall probability of being accepted to at least one medical school (if you apply across the board) is about 40%. Not bad. The figure of 2% comes from the fact that every applicant applies to more than one school, giving the illusion that there are far more applicants than available positions. Thus, your chance of being accepted to at least one medical school after applying to 20 is actually higher than 33%, because the number of applicants is far fewer than the number of applications received by medical schools.

Our goal here is not to turn you into a statistician or a gambler, but to stress the point that all the hard work in the world won't get you admitted if you don't apply intelligently. You must be fully aware of how to increase your odds—which usually means submitting as many applications as possible. As Dean Dodson advises, "Apply early; apply often—like voting in Chicago."

Deciding Where to Apply

Students with high grades and MCAT scores will likely have a wide choice of medical schools to attend. However, they are a minority, because most students usually get accepted to only one or two schools. Therefore, it's critical that you choose the correct schools to which to apply.

We recommend that you divide the number of schools you plan to apply to into quarters and rank them on their relative appeal. (The end of the chapter has a ranking of schools.) The first quarter should include schools where you never expect to get accepted but would attend instantly if you did (e.g., Harvard). The second quarter should include the very competitive schools, then the strong schools, and the final fourth should be all the rest.

For example, if you apply to 20 schools, you would choose five schools from each of the four groups at the end of the chapter. By spreading yourself out like this, you will increase your odds of acceptance and might get some nice surprises.

You should consider whether the school is public or private. Typically, about 68% of medical students attend schools in their home states. In general, public schools accept mostly state residents, so applying to the Univ. of Tennessee when you live in Connecticut could be a total waste of time.

On the other hand, such a rule can work to your advantage. In some states, especially in the Midwest, the number of in-state applicants is so small that the public medical schools have trouble filling their classes.

Therefore, nearly every state resident who applies gets in, so the admission requirements are much lower than at private schools. If you move to one of these states and establish residency, you have an almost guaranteed acceptance to the state medical school. Of course, this ploy is drastic and should be a last resort.

Another thing to determine is the school's acceptance ratio (how many students it accepts versus how many apply). Of course, you'll want to look for the best ratio. *Medical School Admission Requirements* has all this data.

Other important questions to consider:

1. Do you like the location?

Although you'll probably attend whatever school you get in—and you should never eliminate schools in your home state—it doesn't hurt to at least consider location before applying. There are many medical schools in many different locales, so you shouldn't have to settle for a place where you'll be miserable.

2. What are the clinical and research facilities like?

This is very important, because it will give you an indication of what types of patients you'll see and how many you'll see. In general, county and city hospitals see much more action, courtesy of the local "knife and gun clubs," than private hospitals. The number of patients the hospital treats annually will also indicate how much clinical experience you'll get. If you want to become involved in research, find out the amount and type of research conducted at that school.

3. How is the education delivered?

Find out how many days per week—and how many hours per day—you're in school. Most medical schools go five days a week; some go four or six. Some have nine hours of class per day; others average only four. Some schools provide note-taking services; others make you struggle on your own. Some ease the tension by having a pass/fail grading system; others can be cutthroat and neurotic with letter grades. Interactive software and virtual reality are making education more fun at some schools, including Loma Linda, U.C. San Diego, N.Y.U., and Cornell. The curriculum may not seem important to you now, when all you're thinking about is "Will I get in?" but these points are critical, because they can make the difference between an exciting learning experience and an awful one.

4. What about housing and health benefits?

High-quality, low-cost dormitories or subsidized housing can greatly affect your overall expenses, especially at urban schools. Living in a cockroach-infested apartment won't help your study habits much, either. Make sure to see the "typical" student housing and determine if housing is guaranteed for all four years. Health benefits are an important but often overlooked issue. Students are not employees and are not covered by employee health and disability programs. For instance, will prophylactic AZT be available in the event of an HIV-infected needle-stick? Does the school provide the hepatitis B vaccine free? On a more mundane level, will you have to spend your hard-earned student loan money on dental work or contact lenses?

Financial Aid for Medical School

It sounds implausible, but it's true: your finances should not restrict your choice of medical school. Once you are accepted, the school will work with you to ensure that you and your family will be able to pay tuition and still live comfortably.

All medical schools inform students about the Stafford Loan program (formerly the Guaranteed Student Loan), Health Education Assistance Loan (HEAL), Supplemental Loan for Students (SLS), Perkins Loan, Homan Loan, University Loans, and various state programs. Also, be sure to note the federally-funded Armed Forces Scholarship and the Medical Scientist Training Program (MSTP), which is open to all and pays tuition plus stipend (see below). First- and second-year minority students should get information about the National Medical Fellowships.

There are many more scholarship and loan programs—too many to list here. The bottom line is, your medical school's financial aid office will help you meet the high cost of your education.

Don't worry too much about signing for loans, either. Despite the fact that the average total debt for a recent graduating class was over $80,000 per student, you'll eventually be able to repay the loans for your tuition pretty easily. Skeptical? To convince you, we've listed below the average salaries of various specialties, according to a survey published by *Modern Healthcare* in 1998:

Specialty	Mean Compensation
Anesthesiology	$203,326
Cardiology	$207,690
Emergency Medicine	$157,286
Family Practice	$122,625
General Surgery	$190,273
Internal Medicine	$127,366
Neurology	$149,309
Obstetrics/Gynecology	$204,752
Oncology	$173,655
Pathology	$175,048
Pediatrics	$121,776
Psychiatry	$130,267
Radiology	$209,150

Since we've raised the issue of earnings potential, we feel we should remind you that good medicine always requires the doctor to place the patients' needs first. If your goal is to make a ton of money in as little time as possible, go into investment banking. You'll be happier and society will benefit more. If your concern is how you're ever going to repay your medical school loans, relax. There's no denying that you may face a short-term struggle, especially while subsisting on a resident's salary. And you may have to wait a little longer than your business school friends to buy a house or a Porsche. But if you're enjoying your profession and making a positive difference in people's lives, the struggle is well worth it.

Final Review of Your Application

A few more points to consider before you mail that AMCAS application:

1. Make a final check for absolute accuracy and neatness.

2. Have other people read what you've written. Your premedical advisor, a premedical friend, or the family physician are good choices, since they are familiar with the process. An English teacher can help with style or grammar problems.

3. Make sure you use the entire space (with reasonably sized print and margins, of course) for personal comments, and try to

be original. For example, don't write about how you've wanted to be a doctor since you were a kid. This was everyone's ambition at age four. Most applicants will spend months working on their essays before they write the final version, so get started way in advance. We'll discuss the essay in greater depth in Chapter 6.

4. Photocopy the application and keep it in a safe place in case AMCAS loses it, and also for interview preparation.

5. Always send the application via certified mail if you are approaching a deadline. This will put the burden of explanation on AMCAS should the application be lost.

After You've Applied

Once you file your application, it will be just a matter of time before you receive requests for interviews. In the meantime, it's important that you follow up on your application.

For starters, keep a meticulous record of your status at each school. We recommend making a chart with your schools in one column and receipt of application, secondary application, interview, etc. in other columns. Write in the date when each category is filled. This way, you' know if a school seems overdue for a note or phone call from you.

It's perfectly acceptable to phone schools. Of course, you don't what to harass them, but calling occasionally to determine the status of your application is a good idea, since applications do get lost and letters of recommendation misplaced. If you try to be extremely cordial on the phone, you may find yourself on a first-name basis with the secretaries. This may sound unimportant, but one applicant got to know the secretary well enough that she hand-carried his application to the Dean of Admissions at U.C. Davis. The fax machine can be another very useful tool.

If you're not accepted right away, don't panic and ruin your senior year of college. Some applicants will receive acceptance letters in the fall, but most are accepted in the spring.

Often, half of an entering medical class comes from the waiting list, so don't get discouraged if you are wait-listed. If several schools put you on a waiting list, the odds are good you'll get into at least one, since these lists are usually about twice as large as the actual entering class.

As you wait to hear from schools, have an answering machine or someone always available to receive messages, especially as you approach the end of summer and the beginning of medical school registration. Be sure to notify the schools if your address or phone number changes.

Also, keep the admissions department abreast of any new awards, publications, etc. that may strengthen your application. (However, sending new transcripts, unless they are dramatically improved, is usually not helpful.) Here's a good example: A student had planned to matriculate at his second-choice school. The week before classes began, he was in the newspaper for placing third in a balloon race. He mailed the article to his first-choice school and drew an arrow to himself in the newspaper photograph saying, "Please, pick me up!" The school called him the day before classes began and offered him admission. After partying on Bourbon Street in New Orleans, he sped north to New York City—another happy ending.

Handling Acceptances

Students usually begin collecting letters of acceptance at their safety schools first. According to the rules of the game, applicants may not hold more than one acceptance offer after May 15. If you're waiting to compare financial aid packages, make sure to contact the schools involved and apprise them of this before the deadline.

This rule can make things tricky. For example, one applicant was holding acceptances to four schools when a Director of Admissions threatened to retract his acceptance if the applicant didn't decide soon. (All AMCAS-participating schools know your status at the other schools to which you applied.) After being confronted, the student rushed to the post office and declined admission at three of the four schools. For the fourth school, he quickly filled out and mailed the registration form weeks early—thereby committing himself to that school.

A few days later, Johns Hopkins (a better school than any of the original four that had accepted him) learned that the applicant was now holding only one spot, and they offered him a place. Unfortunately, Johns Hopkins had to retract the offer when they discovered that the student had officially registered at another school.

The lesson: don't hold multiple acceptances, but don't rush to register at any school early.

Special Programs*

Medical Scientist Training Program (MSTP): The National Institutes of Health (NIH) provides funding to students who wish to pursue scientific and medical training (M.D.-Ph.D.) at the schools listed below. Each year, approximately 150 new students receive scholarships that pay an annual stipend of $10,000 plus tuition. After training, the student is obligated to conduct research or teach, usually for five years. For more information on the MSTP, contact:

> **National Institute of Health**
> **MSTP Program Administrator**
> **Room 905, Westwood Building**
> **Bethesda, MD 20892**
> **(phone 301-594-7744)**

Another 81 schools offer the option of obtaining a combined M.D.-Ph.D. degree, but these programs aren't funded by the NIH. Some are funded privately; others aren't funded at all. Information on these programs usually comes with the medical school's application. The NIH-supported programs are now at these schools:

Albert Einstein	**U.C. San Diego**
Baylor	**U.C. San Francisco**
Case Western Reserve	**U. Chicago**
Columbia	**U. Colorado**
Cornell	**U. Iowa**
Duke	**U. Michigan**
Emory	**U. Minnesota**
Harvard	**U. Pennsylvania**
Johns Hopkins	**U. Pittsburgh**
Mount Sinai	**U. Rochester**
New York U.	**U. Texas Southwestern (Dallas)**
Northwestern	**U. Virginia**
Stanford	**U. Washington**
SUNY Stony Brook	**Vanderbilt**
Tufts	**Washington U. (St. Louis)**
U. Alabama/Birmingham	**Yale**
UCLA	

*Data from **Medical School Admissions Requirements**, published by the Association of American Medical Colleges.

B.A./B.S.-M.D. Programs: Some schools offer the chance to combine undergraduate and medical training. This program, usually six years, lets students avoid most of the anxiety of the medical school application process. Some programs operate in combination with several undergraduate colleges. The following schools offer this program:

Albany Medical College
Allegheny Univ. of the Health Sciences
Baylor College of Medicine
Boston Univ.
Brown Univ.
Case Western Reserve
Chicago Medical School
City Univ. of New York
East Tennessee State
Eastern Virginia Medical School
George Washington Univ.
Howard Univ. (Washington, DC)
LSU (Shreveport, New Orleans)*
Meharry Medical College
Michigan State Univ.
New York Univ.
Northeastern (Ohio)
Northwestern Univ.
Penn State Univ.
SUNY Brooklyn
SUNY Syracuse
Thomas Jefferson
Univ. Alabama, Birmingham
UCLA
USC
UMDNJ (Robert Wood Johnson, NJ Medical)
Univ. Miami*
Univ. Michigan
Univ. Missouri, Kansas City
Univ. Rochester
Univ. South Alabama
Univ. Wisconsin, Madison*

*Program limited to state residents.

M.D.-J.D. Programs: These programs let medical students pursue a law degree as well as an M.D. These schools offer this option:

> **Duke**
> **Southern Illinois Univ.**
> **Univ. of Chicago**
> **Univ. Illinois (Urbana, Champaign)**
> **Univ. of Pennsylvania**
> **Yale Univ.**
> **West Virginia Univ.**

M.D.-M.B.A. Programs: These schools allow medical students to get a business school degree with their M.D.:

> **Allegheny Univ. of the Health Sciences**
> **Case Western Reserve**
> **Dartmouth**
> **Thomas Jefferson**
> **UCLA**
> **Univ. of Chicago**
> **Univ. Illinois (Urbana, Champaign)**
> **Univ. of Pennsylvania**
> **Vanderbilt Univ.**
> **Wake Forest Univ.**

Timetable of Important Dates

JUNIOR YEAR

NOVEMBER THROUGH APRIL:
- Begin review for MCAT's.

FEBRUARY OR MARCH:
- Apply for April MCAT.

APRIL:
- Compile a list of medical schools to apply to.
- Collect letters of recommendation.
- Suggested time to take MCAT.
- Get the AMCAS application packet from your advisor or AMCAS, or download AMCAS-E from the web site.
- Write first draft of AMCAS essay.

MAY:
- Interpret MCAT scores and GPA with premedical advisor (see note below).
- Send for medical school catalogs and non-AMCAS applications.
- Check a copy of your transcript to make sure your grades are accurate.
- Send transcripts to AMCAS and non-AMCAS schools.
- Revise and polish AMCAS essay.

JUNE:
- Submit AMCAS application at earliest allowed date.
- Complete non-AMCAS applications as soon as possible.

JULY:
- Register for fall MCAT if your previous scores were low and you think you are now better prepared.
- If your school has a premedical committee, tell them where to send your composite recommendation letter.

AUGUST:
- Take August MCAT, if necessary.

SENIOR YEAR

SEPTEMBER:
- Make sure that your applications are complete and that letters of recommendation have been received. Call to confirm if necessary.

NOVEMBER:
- Be patient—interviews will come!

DECEMBER:
- Try to schedule interviews during Winter Break for convenience.

JANUARY:
- Fill out GAPSFAS form for financial aid and investigate other financial aid sources.
- Send updated transcripts if requested by schools.

FEBRUARY:
- If no one loves you by Valentine's Day, speak immediately with your premedical advisor. He or she may be able to call on your behalf.

MARCH:
- If you are wait-listed, send a letter to the school and express your continued interest.

APRIL THROUGH AUGUST:
- Schools are still sending acceptance letters, so stay calm. Make sure medical schools can reach you or a family member by telephone at all times.

Note: Keep in mind that a few undergraduate programs like to boast "our acceptance rate to medical school is 80%" because it sounds impressive to high school students. (That is, students and parents are more willing to pay the high tuition the school demands because they think they'll definitely get into medical school from that college.)

In reality, the acceptance rate is so high because the school does a student weed-out. They tell mediocre pre-meds that their chances of getting into medical school are horrible, so they shouldn't even apply to med school, when in fact they may have a reasonable chance of acceptance. So the only students who apply are stars who will get in easily—thus giving the high acceptance rate.

The lesson here is simple: take your premedical advisor's counseling with a grain of salt. Ultimately, the decisions should be yours alone.

Ranking U.S. Medical Schools

The medical schools below are divided into four categories to help you make a rational decision about where to apply. The groups are based on the *U.S. News & World Report Best Graduate Schools* and the eighth edition of *The Gourman Report* by Jack Gourman, Ph.D. For the record, the AAMC discourages medical schools from participating in the *U.S. News* survey, so view the rankings with some skepticism. Many people also consider *The Gourman Report* flawed, since Dr. Gourman makes no attempt to explain his ranking methodology.

Reputation still means a lot in the world of medicine, however, no matter what it's based upon. As a compromise, we've listed the schools in general categories rather than with absolute rankings.

The Top 25

Albert Einstein College of Medicine
Baylor College of Medicine
Case Western Reserve University
Columbia University College of Physicians & Surgeons
Cornell University Medical College
Duke University
Emory University
Harvard University
Johns Hopkins University
Mayo Medical School
New York University
Northwestern University
Stanford University
University of California—Los Angeles
University of California—San Diego
University of California—San Francisco
University of Chicago
University of Michigan
University of Pennsylvania
University of Pittsburgh
University of Texas Southwestern Medical Center at Dallas
University of Washington
Vanderbilt University
Washington University
Yale University

Very Competitive

Brown University
Boston University
Dartmouth Medical School
George Washington University
Georgetown University
Indiana University
Loma Linda University
Loyola University of Chicago
Ohio State University
Saint Louis University
State University of New York—Buffalo
State University of New York—Stony Brook
Temple University
Tufts University
Tulane University
University of California—Davis
University of California—Irvine
University of Illinois
University of Iowa
University of Louisville
University of Minnesota—Minneapolis
University of Missouri—Columbia
University of North Carolina at Chapel Hill
University of Rochester
University of Southern California
University of Virginia
University of Wisconsin
Wake Forest University
Wayne State University

Competitive

Albany Medical College
Creighton University
Louisiana State University—New Orleans
Louisiana State University—Shreveport
Michigan State University

Mount Sinai School of Medicine
Oregon Health Sciences University
Pennsylvania State University
State University of New York—Brooklyn
State University of New York—Syracuse
University of Alabama—Birmingham
University of Cincinnati
University of Colorado
University of Connecticut
University of Florida
University of Kansas—Kansas City
University of Kentucky
University of Maryland
University of Miami
University of Missouri—Kansas City
University of Nebraska
University of Tennessee
University of Texas—Galveston
University of Texas—San Antonio
University of Utah
University of Vermont

Good

Most everywhere else.

(Interestingly, Dr. Gourman does not rank any U.S. medical school below his "Acceptable Plus" category, as he does for some other professional and graduate degree programs.)

Another Option: Osteopathic Medicine

Not all doctors have an "M.D." An alternate path is D.O., or doctor of osteopathic medicine. D.O.s practice in all 50 states, about 60% of them in primary care specialties.

Listed below are the 18 osteopathic medical colleges in the U.S. On average, their prerequisite GPA may be a bit lower, and the tuition a bit higher. Ask your premed advisor for more information and check the AACOM (osteopathic version of the AAMC) web site at www.aacom.org.

Arizona College of Osteopathic Medicine
Chicago College of Osteopathic Medicine
Kirksville College of Osteopathic Medicine
Lake Erie College of Osteopathic Medicine
Michigan State University College of Osteopathic Medicine
New York College of Osteopathic Medicine
Nova Southeastern University College of Osteopathic
    Medicine (Ft. Lauderdale)
Ohio University College of Osteopathic Medicine
Oklahoma State University College of Osteopathic Medicine
Philadelphia College of Osteopathic Medicine
Pikeville College School of Osteopathic Medicine
Touro University College of Osteopathic Medicine (San Francisco)
The University of Health Sciences—College of Osteopathic
    Medicine (Kansas City)
University of Medicine and Dentistry of New Jersey School of
    Osteopathic Medicine
University of New England College of Osteopathic Medicine
University of North Texas Health Science Center—Texas College
    of Osteopathic Medicine
University of Osteopathic Medicine and Health Sciences (Des Moines)
West Virginia School of Osteopathic Medicine
Western University of the Health Sciences/College
    of Osteopathic Medicine of the Pacific (Pomona)

The Nation's Best Hospitals*

1. Johns Hopkins Hospital — Baltimore, MD
2. Mayo Clinic — Rochester, MN
3. Massachusetts General Hospital — Boston, MA
4. Duke University Medical Center — Durham, NC
5. UCLA Medical Center — Los Angeles, CA
6. Cleveland Clinic — Cleveland, OH
7. Stanford University Hospital — Stanford, CA
8. Brigham and Women's Hospital — Boston, MA
9. Barnes-Jewish Hospital — St. Louis, MO
10. UCSF Medical Center — San Francisco, CA
11. Hospital of the University of Pennsylvania — Philadelphia, PA
12. University of Chicago Hospitals (tie) — Chicago, IL
    University of Michigan Medical Center (tie) — Ann Arbor, MI
14. University of Washington Medical Center — Seattle, WA

*According to *U.S. News & World Report*, 1998.

5

THE INTERVIEW

*F*OR APPLICANTS WITH GOOD GRADES and MCAT scores, the interview is often just a formality. But for most students, it is a critical part of the admissions process.

The purpose of the interview is to obtain information independent of and supplementary to the data you supplied on the application. An interviewer may assess a candidate's academic potential, maturity, motivation, leadership, interests, knowledge of medicine, attitude, ability to relate to others, and other subjective criteria. A strong interview can increase your chance of admission tremendously, and a bad one can destroy even the class valedictorian. Therefore, it's essential that you understand the ingredients of a good interview.

We believe interviewing is a skill you can learn. But, of course, it's impossible for us to teach you through a book. Improvement requires personal interaction. For example, if you think you may be perceived as shy, arrogant, goofy, or whatever, ask a friend or your premedical advisor to conduct mock

The real art of conversation is not only to say the right thing in the right place, but to leave unsaid the wrong thing at the tempting moment.

—Dorothy Nevill

interviews with you. It's an excellent way to improve your interviewing skills.

Better yet, use a video camera and VCR to study yourself as you answer questions. The tape will give you a realistic picture of how others perceive you. There are even courses designed to teach interviewing skills, but don't bother taking them unless you have a major problem (e.g., extreme shyness) to overcome.

The Interview Process

In general, the interview process is divided into three parts: the orientation, the tour, and the actual interview.

Not every school offers an orientation, but most do. Its purpose is not to evaluate applicants, but to inform them about what the day will entail.

All the other applicants to be interviewed will be with you at the orientation. Some may try to give you the impression that they are totally superior or that they were Albert Einstein in a past life or something. Don't pay any attention to them. They're just playing mind games with you and trying to mess with their competition. Just remain pleasant and smile a lot. Your display of maturity will probably bug them more than anything else you could do.

Use the orientation as a time to relax and gather your thoughts. Remember, if you are asked for an interview, it means they want you as much as you want them. Their goal for that day will be to sell you on their school and convince you to attend it over other schools that might accept you.

The Tour

After the orientation, you'll tour the medical school. The tour, which will cover the clinical and instructional facilities, is when you'll get the big sales pitch. Many applicants get so anxious about their interview that they forget that the school is really the one under scrutiny. Contrary to popular opinion, one medical school is not like the next. Each has a unique personality, which you may or may not like.

A medical student who has no bearing whatsoever on admissions decisions usually gives the tour, so feel free to ask any questions. It's essential that you take time in the tour to get a feel for the school, in case you must decide between two or more schools.

For this reason, unless lack of funds totally prohibits travel, never accept the option to be interviewed in your area rather than at the school. Many schools send a representative to, say, California to interview applicants who can't afford (or just don't want) to fly east.

If you can, spend the night before the interview with a medical student. He/she will usually offer good insight about what things are really like at the school.

The Interview

Your interviewers will usually be two faculty members, or a faculty member and a medical student. In the latter case, the faculty member will carry more weight, but don't underestimate the input from the student. Acting like he/she is a peon in the admissions process will guarantee your rejection. The faculty interview may help you get in, while the medical student interview can weed you out.

Again, either or both may be on the admissions committee, so it's not a good idea to say anything too bizarre. Instead, the interview is your chance to expand on information that may not be clear to the committee. Applications do not have room for great detail, and they force the applicant to abbreviate and oversimplify. Just remember to be yourself, since it's usually easy for an experienced interviewer to tell if someone is lying or exaggerating.

Some schools turn the interview into a contest. At Northwestern and Emory (or so the rumor mills report), a few students are lined up and interrogated as a group by a panel of admissions officers. Although this can be an intimidating and somewhat impersonal situation, you can benefit by using the time when other applicants are talking to formulate a better response of your own.

Many people tell horror stories of how a "friend of a friend" had a doctor give him a hard time in an interview. Though it's possible you'll encounter a jerk, most interviewers want to make the experience as stress-free as possible. Don't forget—the interviewer has been through the same thing and will be aware of (and usually sympathetic to) your nervousness.

One of our classmates did have a real hard time in one interview. At the end, the doctor said, "Sorry I was so hard on you, but it's only because I really want to recommend you. I wanted to be sure you had the right stuff. If I don't want somebody, I usually just give him a real easy interview." The moral: don't judge what the interviewer thinks of you by the way you're treated in the interview. Sometimes, they just want to see how you react to a stressful situation.

For example, there's an interviewer at a Texas school who shakes your hand, smiles, and asks, "So, how many times a week do you masturbate?" A friend of ours answered, without missing a beat, "Not as much as I deserve." Another friend was asked, "When are you going to get married?" To which she replied, "Is this a proposal?" Yet another female friend was asked, "Once you get married, how will your husband feel about your palpating another man's scrotum?" Her reply was calm and professional.

Interviewers ask such questions only to see how you react to very personal or taboo subjects. Reacting with humor or maturity is far wiser than getting angry or upset. Remember, a physician must handle complex moral and ethical issues—and all types of patient personalities—in a dignified, tactful manner.

Then there are interviewers who just like to hear themselves talk. They want to impress you with how much they think they know. All you have to do is be a good listener, seem interested, and be patient. It'll be over soon.

Finally, if you don't know an answer to a question, just say, "I don't know." Nothing sounds worse than someone fumbling to make up an answer.

Final Preparation before the Interview

You probably know the cliche, "You get only one chance to make a first impression." And given the volume of applicants that interviewers must see, the first impression is often the only impression. This means that for men, a suit, and for women, a conservative dress or suit, are mandatory. And don't neglect grooming. Get a haircut, trim your beard, clean your fingernails, etc. We don't mean to sound like your mom, but the informality of dorm life at college can make you forget how people dress and behave in the real world.

Before the interview, review your photocopy of the application you sent to the school. Often, interviewers will ask you to clarify or elaborate on something in your application. Chances are, you filled it out months ago, and if you don't review it, you probably won't remember what the point was. This looks bad.

Also, read the catalog the school sent you. Having a little substantive knowledge about the school is a compliment to the interviewer and looks impressive.

Above all, remember to pronounce the interviewer's name correctly, since you'll want to say, "Thank you, Dr. Radiziewski. It's been a pleasure speaking with you," or whatever. No sound is more important to people than the sound of their own names. In medical school, interviews, and life in general, always refer to people by their names. It makes them feel, consciously or subconsciously, important—and they'll remember your kindness.

Being polite and personal also helps with the secretaries in the admissions office. More than one applicant has been derailed by being rude to the secretary. Secretaries often attend the final admissions committee meetings, and since they have likely met all the applicants, they may occasionally make a negative statement—guaranteed to sink that student. No medical college wants someone who brown-noses professors and physicians while treating nurses, secretaries, and administrators with contempt. Besides, being on a friendly basis with the secretaries can help tremendously when you are curious about the status of your application.

Sample Interview Questions

Your interviewers will ask a variety of questions, and your answers should demonstrate your maturity, character, knowledge, and ability to communicate. There's really no way to "study" for an interview, but for curiosity's sake, we've compiled a list of questions asked in actual interviews. You may not get similar questions, but it might be useful just for practice to think about how you would answer them.

How do you know that medicine is for you?

What has been your most important accomplishment?

Do you think doctors are viewed with as much respect today as in the past?

Is medicine becoming more technical, and is this beneficial?

What do you think of euthanasia? Abortion? Cloning?

What can be done about rising health-care costs?

If a 15-year-old girl comes to you and wants birth control pills, what would you tell her?

How do you feel about animal research?

What do you think about the current push to limit the number of specialty residency positions?

Tell me about your research work. (Be sure you understand thoroughly any lab work you've participated in, no matter how small your role.)

What are your strong points? Your weaknesses? Your hobbies?

Are you interested in any specialties?

What will you do if you don't get accepted to medical school?

Why do you want to work with sick people?

Do you think doctors are overpaid?

Do you feel you are prepared to enter medical school?

Why did you apply to this school? What other schools did you apply to? Why?

How will you finance your education?

Tell us about your undergraduate institution.

When did you decide to become a doctor?

Would you consider applying to a foreign medical school if you were rejected by all the U.S. schools?

Are admissions quotas fair?

Are you concerned about the surplus of doctors that's supposed to occur when you begin practicing?

What makes you different from everyone else?

What three adjectives best describe you?

What do you see yourself doing ten years from now? (A very popular question. Unfortunately, one student answered, "Uh, this is Wednesday, about two o'clock, right?" The interviewer said, "Yes, it is." The student swung his arm up as if he were holding a golf club and said, "I should be on the eighth hole." Apparently, his humor wasn't appreciated—he was rejected by that school.)

Where would you go to medical school, given the choice?

How do you intend to integrate medical school (or your medical practice) and your family/social life?

What do you do for fun?

Describe your relationship with your family.

What do you know about hospices, HMO's, or PPO's?

What do you expect to get from a career in medicine?

Do you have any children, or plan to? (This is actually an illegal question, and female applicants are asked it far more often than males. But this is not the time to start quoting the law. Just give a straightforward answer and try not to act offended.)

Which course would you recommend all students take?

How will you prepare for medical school between now and the fall?

What books have you read recently?

What is your favorite piece of music?

What do you think happens to you after you die?

If you were in charge of an HMO, would you choose to cover organ donations or infertility treatments?

How would your best friend describe you?

If you had six months to do whatever you wanted to, what would it be?

If you had unlimited access to money for a week, what would you do?

How would you deal with a non-English-speaking patient?

How would you rank three qualities of a physician in importance: compassion, integrity, and medical knowledge? Why?

If you could have dinner with any three people from history, who would they be? (A classic.)

What questions do you have? (You could ask: What do you think are this school's weaknesses and how are they being improved? What research opportunities would I have? How is your school unique? How would you describe the typical class personality here? and so on.)

6

THE ESSAY

....

SO YOUR TRANSCRIPT IS COMPLETE, the MCAT is over, and you are now completing the AMCAS application. At this point, your immediate goal is to get an interview.

As we have already noted, some applicants will be rejected immediately because their scores and grades are too low, while others are almost guaranteed interviews because of their amazing numbers. For students between these two extremes (probably most of you), nothing is stamped in concrete, and a good essay can earn an interview. On the other hand, an excellent applicant who writes a sloppy essay or a weird piece about how his parents are pressuring him into medicine may in fact be writing his own rejection letter.

Everyone has an image of the "good physician," and, fair or not, you will be measured against this image. While ambition and intellect are important, the committee is also seeking students who are compassionate, sensitive, and committed to medicine. Your essay should help the interviewers develop this image of you, and you can expect them to read your essay before the interview or immediately afterwards.

Following this chapter are actual AMCAS essays by medical students accepted at Cornell, Johns Hopkins, Yale, Harvard, Columbia, Univ. of Pennsylvania, Washington University, U.T. Southwestern, and other top schools. We believe these pieces will give you a feel for the creativity and self-description that defines a successful essay, and we hope they will be a catalyst for your own creativity.

We have intentionally mixed exceptional essays with more ordinary pieces to illustrate a simple point: even applicants with mediocre essays get into top medical schools. Of course, you should try to model your essay after the best presented here. To help you, we will comment briefly on the strengths and weaknesses of representative essays.

Authorship, Proofreading, and Style

This section addresses two important points. First, the ideas and writing style should be yours and yours alone. If you have not internalized a philosophy of medicine—and developed a coherent way of expressing it—you will fumble in the interview.

Second, your message is more important than your writing style, but don't make a bad impression with convoluted prose and sloppiness. Deans of Admission assume your essay was proofread by Mom, Dad, a professor, a premedical advisor, and six or seven roommates, so don't hesitate to ask someone to check at least your spelling and grammar.

Essay #1 is extremely well written. The applicant clearly communicates her ideas and convinces the reader she has thought maturely about her goals. You can bet the interviewer asked her more about her view of life and her experiences with hematology/oncology and counseling.

The writing style in Essay #19 is unique. It shouts the applicant's enthusiasm and excitement about entering medicine and enjoying life. He takes the reader on a trip to the ocean, classroom, kitchen, subway, frat house, forest, and physician's office. He does not follow another's path or force himself into the premedical mold. Rather, he presents himself as a naturalist, idealist, and romantic.

If the writer of Essay #2 had not been accepted to medical school, she could have made a living as a book or movie critic. The beginning of the essay conjures vivid images of the doctor and disease, and we are left feeling that the applicant is the humanitarian. In fact, we feel she is talking about herself when she writes, "through close reading, the author's philosophy of life can be discovered." Not only does she recognize the value of a liberal arts education, she personalizes her view of medicine.

The best essays attract attention with an opening sentence that grabs the reader, draws him into the piece, and ties together the rest of the work. In journalism, it's called a "good lead." Examples include

Essay #46—"If you don't get paid, why the Hell do you work here?"

Essay #27—"A successful and effective physician must possess two essential qualities—a thirst for knowledge, and a deep motivation to aid his fellow man."

Essay #33—"I love to live. I love to feel the sweat drip down my face as I run the Campus Drive loop."

Essay #42—"Praeludium. In the beginning there was dissonance."

A good lead grabs readers, puts them on your side, and makes them want to read more. It also makes your essay memorable.

Rather than being a hodgepodge of thoughts and achievements, your essay should have a central theme or motif to bridge experiences, concepts, and extracurricular activities. Essay #37 explains the author's dual devotion to literature and medicine, evoking William Carlos Williams both as a role model and theme for the essay. The author of Essay #8 uses "communication" to discuss nature, philosophy of medicine, and life experiences. With society criticizing medical schools for producing impersonal technocrats, a poet who communicates well will stand out from the crowd.

In contrast, Essays #13 and #20 exemplify a subtle mistake in many essays: Applicants begin their essays with an interesting concept, question, or idea, only to stray from the central theme when listing personal achievements. As a result, the body of these essays do not clearly support their leads or conclusions. If at all possible, list your accomplishments elsewhere in the application, or have them described in your letters of recommendation. Use the essay for more personal communication.

Once you've written your final draft, there are only a few standards to follow when typing your essay. Most important, be neat. Check that there are no visible corrections or spelling mistakes. This may seem obvious, but as we read through hundreds of essays to choose 50 for this book, we were shocked at the number of typographical errors. Usually, applicants use a computer or pay to have the essay professionally typed.

The length of the essay can vary widely. Of the essays we reviewed, some were short, such as Essay #11 (under 200 words) and #46 (under 400 words). At the other extreme, #42 exceeded 1,500 words on one page. A successful essay does not have to fill the entire page with print.

It's better to express your feelings and drives succinctly. ("Brevity is the soul of wit."—Thoreau)

There is also no consistency among essays regarding margins, spacing, paragraphing, or font. At the bottom of Essays #40 and #47, the applicants typed and signed their names. This adds a personal touch and authenticity, and may be appropriate for some.

In sum, the successful essay comes in all shapes and sizes, but its appearance and style is not nearly as important as its message.

Conservative and Safe

A conservative and safe essay can still succeed. The author of Essay #21 recognizes that many of the people who will be reading his essay are academic physicians. Saying that he eventually wants "to work in a university affiliated hospital, and to be involved in clinically related research, while maintaining patient contact" is exactly what they want to hear. He stresses he is excited about the field of medicine and believes he will enjoy caring for the sick. He mirrors his reader.

Having stressed the "correct" reasons for entering medicine, he then fills the essay with information and details that are probably interesting to the researcher and impressive to the layman—but they add little (good or bad) to the picture of the applicant as a person. Early in his career, this student apparently decided to follow the Hippocratic Oath: *Primum non nocere* ("Above all, do no harm").

Often, the committee member is looking for students with a sense of balance between humanities and sciences, studies and athletics, work and fun. As an undergraduate, the applicant in Essay #26 balanced "a full dose of the humanities and a strong foundation in the physical sciences"—he majored in both physics and English. The woman in Essay #43 shares, "I also enjoy both listening to and performing music and hope to strike a rewarding balance between personal and professional creativity." In Essay #17, no one could question the applicant's research background. He has published two papers and four abstracts—well above the norm. Further, his proficiency in science is balanced by his artistic talent, national tours, and Broadway performances.

Again, we stress that medical schools are not seeking obsessive/compulsive students willing to lock themselves in a lab for days. Rather, the admissions committee looks for the well-rounded applicant.

The student in Essay #5 conservatively plays the premedical game well: she worked with disadvantaged children, balanced science studies with humanities courses, conducted research at prestigious places, and gained clinical experience. She does not directly say she is a nice person with nice qualities. Instead, she compliments physicians as caring, dedicated, and intelligent. Her essay boosts the ego of the reader—and subtly implies that she shares these attributes. This indirect method is successful.

Creative versus Weird

A creative essay captures the reader's attention with humor or a startling oddness. Since an interviewer reads dozens of essays in one sitting, you want your essay to be remembered—but it must be remembered in a positive way.

Effectively using dialogue, the author of Essay #9 shows he has thought about his goals in clinical medicine and at the laboratory bench. He is inquisitive and motivated, and he realizes there's more to life than straight A's.

Essay #42 won't be forgotten. Organized as a piece of music, the paragraphs are divided into "Praeludium," "Allegro ma non troppo," "Andante," "Adagio," and "Allegro con spirito." Our only criticism of this essay echoes what the King of Austria told Mozart after a performance: "This opera has too many notes."

In your effort to be original, beware of appearing weird or eccentric. Skirting the bizarre, Essay #36 states: "The stories that most appeal to me are of individuals alienated from, or cast into, an alien society, struggling to assert their independence and individuality. By suspending my disbelief, I can partake in the struggle of the fictional characters and feel their victories and defeats." The applicant recognizes that he is challenging psychological norms and continues, "I am careful, however, not to confuse my love of adventure and fantasy with my reasons for wanting to be a physician." However, we wonder whether he would have been so bold if he knew that admissions committees often ask staff psychiatrists to conduct the interview with applicants who write anything unusual in their essays. Take heed.

Apologetic, Egotistical, Doubtful, or Boring

As a rule, don't use the essay to apologize for a low grade or a less than perfect MCAT score, as in #11 or #40. Nobody is perfect, and admissions committees don't want a litany of excuses. They're looking for good reasons to accept you, not trivial reasons to weed you out. Instead, use the space to present positive information about yourself.

Essay #16 comes across as somewhat egotistical, and it exemplifies what *not* to write. There's no question the student has expertise in the lab, and his knowledge of AIDS makes him an attractive candidate. But a commitment to patients should be foremost—and in the first paragraph, not the last line. He should have emphasized his concern in a positive way, not the negative "I will not divorce myself from patient care." He constantly places himself first, and though that may be a characteristic of many ambitious people, it doesn't make for a sympathetic essay. He expresses "realistic concerns for the safety of myself" and anxiety about the AIDS virus appearing in his own low-risk group. He says his greatest satisfaction is in the lab—before he mentions the plight of the AIDS patient. Twice he boasts about receiving strong recommendations and being the only student approved to enter his lab.

Obviously, this applicant has a lot going for him, but his essay is a real turn-off. With a little perspective—that is, put yourself in the readers' shoes—you can appear talented and positive without being arrogant. Allow your credentials to speak for themselves.

One essay we reviewed made a mistake by ending, "The school that accepts me will receive an excited student who will prove to the board of admissions that they did not make a mistake." Although the student wants to leave the committee with the message that he is "excited" about medicine, the reader instead is left wondering why it would be a "mistake" to admit him. What does the applicant feel he has to "prove to the board of admissions" after the fact? Maybe if your entire application is strong, the question is irrelevant, but if there's a weakness in your application, leave it alone.

A mature, appropriate sense of humor never hurts. In Essay #29, the author stresses how his knowledge of microbiology has been useful in his study of gonorrhea. Although probably not intentionally funny, it's a humorous statement. Amuse the reader with mature wit and you will be remembered.

Why a Physician?

Why you decided to become a doctor is a common essay theme. Some students always knew they wanted to be physicians, in the same way children decide they want to be a fireman, a teacher, or President of the United States. The applicant of Essay #40 states that she knew as a child she would be a physician when she grew up, and she discusses how her decision was logically reaffirmed over the years.

However, not every physician chose medicine as a kid playing with a toy stethoscope. The author of Essay #34 cites a single event that sparked his desire to pursue medicine. He then follows this up with more typical experiences as an EMT, bench researcher, and volunteer—all of which solidified his decision. Some students, on the other hand, describe the influence of literature on their decision to pursue medicine. In Essay #3, the student is inspired by Doctor Dolittle and Charles Darwin, while the author of Essay #2 is influenced by a character in *The Plague*.

Professional paths are best decided with maturity and insight. The applicant of Essay #22 began bird-watching in college, had a gut feeling he would enjoy medicine, and tested his interest with clinical, research, and volunteer experiences. He has a good feeling for what lies ahead: "The science may interest me, the diagnoses may challenge me, but it will be that personal involvement with the patient that will make the most difference to me and keep me going through the hardest parts."

Translating Research into Clinical Practice

In general, the most prestigious medical schools emphasize basic research. While only a handful of students actually pursue academic medicine, almost all successful applicants have at least token laboratory experience.

In your essay, you may choose to mention what you did, where you worked, and with whom. In any case, you will want to stress how much you enjoy research (embellish if necessary).

For example, in Essay #33 the student recalls "an incredible high" when his first scientific paper was published. The student in Essay #40 states, "In the long run though, I would like to be a physician who researches medicine on a 'basic science' level and, at the same time, translates advances in scientific theory into clinical practice." Likewise, the applicant in Essay #43 concludes, "I would therefore gain satisfaction from involvement in both the research aspect of medicine and its practical applications in patient care."

Don't panic if you haven't done lab work. You can still mention your dream of pursuing (time permitting) the Nobel Prize in Medicine. And if you aren't convincing, remember that research experience is neither required nor expected at less competitive institutions. Some applicants can get accepted without ever spending a weekend with a pipette, flask, or bunsen burner.

If you really enjoy research, consider the M.D.-Ph.D. programs listed in Chapter 4. If selected, you receive a nice stipend, and your education is completely paid for. (Mom and Dad will love that.) When applying to an intensive joint program like an M.D.-Ph.D., be sure your essay shows balance. Don't discuss research for 99% of the essay and then give one line to medicine. Remember that biomedical research, treating patients, and teaching are three equally important aspects of academic medicine. Essays #17 and #33 make this point well. Nonetheless, the author of Essay #11 is an M.D.-Ph.D. applicant, and his essay addressed only academics (and briefly), but it worked.

Meeting the Physician Shortage

Most medical schools actively recruit qualified minority students who express an interest in serving segments of the population that don't have access to excellent medical care.

In Essay #6, the applicant, a Mexican-American, has considered practicing in a needy Latin American country. He expresses altruistic motives, and he shows scientific aptitude with his authorship on a published paper.

The student in Essay #39 had his interest in medicine sparked after participating in the American Foundation for Negro Affairs Program. Later, he worked in a hematology department testing for sickle cell anemia.

The applicant in Essay #29 states, "My ethnic background has been a contributing factor in my prospective plans after medical school. I would like to work in a physician shortage area where my Puerto Rican background will be helpful in dealing with other Hispanic minorities." She believes it is her "duty in life" to care for others. Essay #44 was also written by a Hispanic who has worked with the poor.

Women as a group have been underrepresented in medicine. Since medicine has been a male-dominated profession, the female doctor sometimes confronts sexist attitudes. The woman in Essay #32 states, "Medicine was a serious consideration but due to the conservative attitude of my parents and Switzerland, the idea of a woman in medicine was not well supported." More alarming than parental pressures are the many female applicants who tell the story of a male doctor who asked during the interview, "Won't your career be ruined when you have a family?" (But remember, he may only have been trying to rattle them; see Chapter 5 for more details.)

The applicant in Essay #33 has insight into the concerns of many admissions officers about the role of women in medicine. She has chosen to confront sexism by describing her open admiration of a successful female physician. The applicant feels she can balance her professional and personal lives, and she addresses the issue persuasively.

Older students often have gained skills and knowledge in fields that might further medicine. One applicant we know attended Bible college and wants to become a missionary doctor. The applicant in Essay #47 pursued a Ph.D. in psychobiology. We also know students who worked as investment bankers, teachers, scientists, police officers, and even medical school professors before beginning med school.

Admissions committees do not expect applicants to know for certain the field of practice they will enter. However, if you think you want to work in an under-served region or less-popular specialty, say so. The minority student in Essay #7 wants to improve health care for the indigent and the elderly. His interests in academic medicine and public health are admirable, because they are areas of medicine criticized for lacking dedicated physicians. He acknowledges that he has benefitted from special opportunities made available to him, and now he says he's eager to use his background to help society. This applicant also improved his chances for admission by participating in a summer program at his first-choice medical school while applying.

Good medical care is also lacking in many rural areas, where the applicant in Essay #12 wants to practice. She describes how her goals developed and how her interests are consistent with her goals. With admissions committees knowledgeable about the problems facing rural areas, they would hesitate to toss this application into a rejection pile.

Stamina

In the past, endurance was extremely important for medical school admission, and a physical handicap would completely eliminate a student's chance for admission. Today, although most students are in good physical shape, some have speech, vision, or other disabilities.

Athletic involvement is a measure of physical stamina—and, presumably, your ability to withstand long nights in the emergency room. Essay #10, #24, #32, and #45 all describe athletic exploits that indicate physical strength and a well-rounded person.

Mental stamina is equally important, and the admissions committee often respects a tough academic major. This probably accounts for engineers having such good luck with admissions. Essay #31 and #35 were written by engineers. And don't forget other challenging undergraduate majors, as in Essay #41. Statistically, economics majors fare well in the medical school admissions game, too.

In addition to physical stamina and academic rigors, mental outlook is an important indicator used by the admissions committee to assess an applicant's fitness for medicine. In Essay #49, the student shares how asthma has influenced his life and decision to become a physician. The applicant in Essay #30 mentions his father's battle with schizophrenia and how the son matured because of the tragedy. In Essay #43, because the applicant witnessed the death of family members, she felt compelled to do her part to integrate modern science with medicine. Similarly, the applicant in Essay #48 was motivated to pursue medicine after helplessly watching his father's injury.

Witnessing illnesses and deaths are powerful influences. How you cope with tragedy is very much a part of the everyday life of a doctor.

Admissions committees will gain a sense of how you deal with the stresses inherent in medicine by how you respond to other types of adversity or pressures (as in the interview). The applicant in Essay #28 brings attention to her maturity and strength, having independently worked her way through college to achieve her goals. Essay #13 emphasizes the author's successful return to higher education, rather than his past difficulties. (Note: Just because the AMCAS application states that the applicant needs to explain any disciplinary action during college, don't assume you should devote the whole page to details. It's better to mention what you learned or how the adversity has helped you.)

The M.D. Family

Sons and daughters of physicians pervade each medical school class. Historically, this is consistent with the Hippocratic Oath, which instructs the doctor to "regard his offspring as equal ... and to teach them this art if they desire to learn it."

Moreover, doctors' kids know what they're getting into. They know about the stress and its toll on the family. Children of physicians have a more realistic view of medicine, its practice, its demands, and its rewards. The applicant in Essay #18 describes how he went through the process of questioning whether medicine was in fact his destined path. Essay #35 is similar in that regard. Children of physicians also wrote Essay #25, #26, and #45.

Name-Dropping

If you work for someone you know and respect, chances are he or she has many other friends as well. The writers of Essay #33 and #43 describe their role models by name.

The physician mentioned in Essay #1, for example, was known and liked at many of the medical schools to which the student applied. The applicant told us that once she learned that the interviewer and she had a mutual friend, she relaxed and did much better in the interview. It's easier to impress someone who already has a good reason to like you.

Likewise, the applicant in Essay #32 says her husband is at Cornell. Having a spouse at a medical school may help gain the applicant an interview. Med students often write letters on behalf of their spouses, boyfriends, or girlfriends. With a strong applicant, a letter of support may convince an admissions committee that the student will matriculate if offered acceptance. The alternative is a student who might transfer to another school later to join his or her spouse. Admissions committees dislike losing students to other schools and feel guilty about breaking up a family or romance.

The point is, if you have an inside connection, make it known to the committee.

Besides using personal contacts, some applicants will name the school they want to attend in their essay. We think this is a very risky tactic, but the applicant in Essay #47 knows where she wants to go: "I have chosen the Cornell Program due to its newly established PET facility as well as its exceptional reputation in the neurosciences."

We caution that name-dropping may limit your options. Presumably, the candidate in Essay #15 planned to attend Buffalo, Baylor, or Cornell. Experience and the contacts she made working at these schools gave her an edge, but unless you are determined to attend a particular school, don't name-drop. Medical schools won't want to send an acceptance letter to someone they'll probably lose to another school. Remember, you must convince each school that it is among your top choices.

A personal story from Daniel: Many interviewers will ask, "What schools have you interviewed with?" Well, one school that interviewed me was SUNY Buffalo, where the interviewer asked me point-blank which school was my first choice and why. I was tempted to lie and say Buffalo, but I straddled the fence. "I am very interested in Buffalo," I replied, "but I would consider Cornell if I had a choice." After a while, he let me change the subject.

At the end of the hour, he studied my application again while he made me wait for what seemed like an eternity. He then closed my file, tossed my application onto his desk, and said, "Mr. Jones, I do not think you'll be coming here."

I really blew it! I thought. I felt I had nothing to lose, so I challenged him. "What do you mean?" He explained that he thought I'd get into Cornell with no problem. He seemed to overlook that I had not yet interviewed there—a fact foremost in my mind. I reminded him that I liked the people I had met at Buffalo, that I thought the tuition was reasonable, and that I didn't mind the weather. In the end, Buffalo did accept me, but the doctor was right. I got into Cornell.

The lesson: doctors aren't stupid, and the interviewer will know you're lying—or at least being insincere—if you say you're dying to go to Podunk Medical School instead of Yale. So don't lie!

A Word of Warning

As you read the essays, you might be tempted to highlight good lines and incorporate them verbatim into your own essay. Some students, unfortunately, might even want to swipe the whole piece and just "change it around a little."

We hope you realize how incredibly dumb that would be. This has been a popular book for many years. Most admissions officers have read these essays, and they would never admit a plagiarist. Any doubts about your integrity will destroy your application—and your reputation.

About the Essays

When you sit down to write your personal statement, we hope you'll use the essays to inspire your creativity. As you read them, we think you'll be relieved to learn how broad the stylistic range is and how diverse the "acceptable" topics are.

The essays should also assist you as you consider your motivations for entering medicine and try to explain them. We cannot stress enough how important it is to be able to articulate your goals maturely during the interview.

Each essay is reprinted exactly as it was written on the application. We have not corrected syntax, grammar, or punctuation errors. But note that rarely would such corrections be necessary. Occasionally, we have changed proper names and locations to guarantee anonymity.

Finally, we would again like to express our gratitude to all the generous medical students who submitted their essays and to the 50 who allowed us to reprint them.

Send Us Your Successful Essay

We are currently collecting another 50 essays for the next edition of this book, and we would be most grateful if readers would send us a copy of an application essay that worked for them. Receipt of your essay will serve as permission to reproduce and critique it. Names will be changed as necessary to protect the innocent.

Since we probably won't be able to use all the essays we get, we will give preference to students attending the most competitive schools. And, although we can't pay you for your essay, we'll gladly send you a free copy of the next edition of the book if your essay is published.

Please send your AMCAS essay, a copy of your medical school acceptance letter or transcript, and your mailing address to

Stephanie Jones
c/o Mustang Publishing
P.O. Box 770426
Memphis, TN 38177 • USA

FIFTY
SUCCESSFUL
APPLICATION
ESSAYS

E s s a y   # 1

M y mother has told me that as a child my favorite question was "how come?" Rarely content with a simple explanation, I seemed constantly to have pushed my parents to give me more details about the way the world worked. This inquisitiveness, while sometimes the subject of affectionate joking, was always encouraged, even when answers were not available. I learned to value the explorative process as much as any "answer" found, and spent much of my free time discovering meadows and brooks, building imaginary civilizations, or immersing myself in a book. My parents are both English professors, and their love of the humanities has always been a vital part of my life. Although my exposure to the sciences at home was limited, I avidly pursued any outside opportunities to learn about the scientific world, and during my high school years the excitement of scientific discovery began to surpass any previous intellectual experiences I had had. Continuing with the humanities, I began to discover that for me novels and music were a luxury, offering pleasure and release. The happiness I derived from them did not have to be forsaken, but could be continued while I pursued a career in science.

Entering Wesleyan University, I thought I would major in Biology while simultaneously exploring as many other fields as possible, but my actual career goals were still hazy. I had previously acquired a taste for scholarship when I worked at Williams College as an archival assistant, but the somewhat solitary nature of the work had lead me to question my desire for a career devoted exclusively to research. During my first two years at Wesleyan, I took several laboratory courses, and found that although they were extremely time consuming, I was excited by the way classroom concepts came alive in the laboratory. Towards the end of my sophomore year a possible career in medicine first became a reality for me. Much that I valued seemed to be present within this field: the opportunity to acquire scientific knowledge, to do research, and to work with and help people. Seeking summer work that would give me the opportunity to explore medicine and medical research, I was fortunate enough to obtain a position in the Department of Hematology/Oncology at UCLA Hospital, with Dr. Martin Cline.

I am still awed by what occurred that summer. At nineteen, I walked into one of the most exciting and meaningful sectors of research in the country. The discoveries that were made while I worked in Dr. Cline's lab were extraordinary, and because I was an integral part of the functioning lab, I felt like an explorer myself. Since part of my responsibility involved getting cancer samples from the hospital every day, I also spent some time in the operating room and a lot of time in pathology. The exposure to clinical and surgical work was as valuable and stimulating as the research. The work was fascinating, the challenge a bit frightening, but I soon felt at ease in both lab and hospital. All that I had learned seemed to come miraculously together that summer.

The doctors I worked for became my mentors. I had not previously realized that one could be both a clinician and a research scientist, and while I sensed that research alone would not fulfill my needs, I still felt a desire to explore this option further. I looked forward to the research I had arranged to do at Wesleyan on my return. At the same time, however, I wanted more experience working directly with people, and when I went back to school in the fall, I trained to be a "listener" for 8 to 8, a student-run counseling service.

My junior year has been thoroughly enriched by my research and counseling experiences. The 8 to 8 training process was invaluable. Through it I learned a lot about myself—my attributes, faults, and values—and about human psychology. Working for the counseling service has strengthened considerably my conviction that medicine is, for me, an ideal vocation, one that would allow me to unite my scientific interests with the personal satisfaction I gain from helping and working with people. The research I am conducting at Wesleyan has been equally fulfilling. As my research experience has grown, my thought processes have slowly begun to change. Designing experiments, I have realized, requires foresight and a thorough integration of many concepts learned in the classroom, abilities I think are important for a doctor to possess, and that I hope I can continue to develop. This summer, at Brigham and Women's Hospital, I will again be doing research, and look forward to exploring still further the world of the laboratory.

My research experiences have been wonderfully rewarding, and I hope to continue laboratory work both through and after medical school. Clinical practice, however, is fundamentally more important to me, because it brings together my interest in people and my scientific and humanitarian ideals. I feel thoroughly committed to a career in medicine and only hope that I am able to give the profession as much as I think it can give to me.

E s s a y   # 2

T he narrator and hero of Albert Camus' novel, *The Plague*, is a doctor named Bernard Rieux. Amidst the horror of the plague which grips his city, the bureaucratic ineptitude, the religious fanaticism embraced by one character and the bleak existentialism presented by another, Dr. Rieux emerges as an advocate for the strength of human will and love. While the epidemic strikes people dead at random, rendering the efforts of medical science impotent, Rieux refuses to succumb to the belief that life is meaningless and tirelessly fights the plague with what little means he has. Romantic as this scenario sounds, Camus presents it objectively, and the novel's power lies in its almost journalistic reality.

When I read *The Plague* in high school, I was greatly drawn to the character of Rieux because of his humanism and because in the face of the epidemic he as a doctor was the only one who could actively do anything, though not much, to combat the disaster. The impotence which he felt against the plague is what all people must feel against any disease, although in many cases medicine can help a great deal. I had some contact with disease and injury while volunteering at a children's hospital in Cleveland. The patients ranged in age from two to twenty, and I visited them in their rooms, played games with or read to them, or just talked. I was glad to be able to give some emotional aid, but I felt powerless to change their condition. The dynamic power of medical science seemed very appealing to me during that experience.

However, as Camus illustrates through Dr. Rieux, being a physician involves more than scientific knowledge and its application. True sympathy—the ability to place oneself in the position of another—is what Rieux achieves and is what makes him a great doctor. I feel that studying literature is one of the best means of expanding one's sympathy. Not only does reading literature require an immersion in the emotional world of the characters, but through close reading, the author's philosophy of life can be discovered. This interpretation is what makes literature so challenging; the ideas are often not explicitly defined. I decided to major in English because I wanted an opportunity to study literature in depth and be able to discuss it with classmates and professors.

In addition to literature, I have taken many history courses, which I feel are equally as important to a liberal arts education. Knowing history helps one to place current social issues in perspective. Most of the history courses I have taken touched upon issues relevant to medicine and society. In an English history course, for example, I read about physicians in the eighteenth century who stole corpses from the gallows for anatomical dissection, because the supply of cadavers for research was strictly controlled by the government. The outrage of witnesses to this practice is paralleled by current public concern about the ethics of medical research, especially in the field of genetics. In my American history courses we covered topics ranging from the unrecognized outbreaks of malaria and typhus which killed many of the first settlers at Jamestown, to the establishment of Medicare under Lyndon Johnson. Studying history makes one aware of the tremendous advances in medical science, and also of the continuity of human attitudes towards medicine.

My own belief that humanism is vital to being a physician was reinforced during the summer I spent working in the Euclid Clinic. I helped patients settle their accounts and fill out insurance forms, so I had a great deal of patient contact. Most of the patients I saw had come directly from a doctor's office, and many of them wanted to talk about their visit. A frequent complaint which I heard was that their doctors rarely took time to listen to questions and worries, or give explanations and reassurance. The patients felt a need to tell someone about their illness or injury, and I spent a lot of time listening. My experience that summer left me with the feeling that although scientific skill may be the most important quality in a doctor, it is not the only necessary quality.

E s s a y # 3

I want to become a physician to heal people and to further my study of man as both creative thinker and purely biological animal. I think I've always been sensitive to the needs of others, and my experiences of the past few years have indicated to me that as a medical doctor I can make the progressive social contribution that is one of my life goals.

As a child I was preoccupied with things biological. I remember digging patiently among ants in their tunnels and trying to locate the eggs, capturing different bees from flowers, attempting to raise bird chicks fallen from their nests, and poring over slides of my blood and hair with a small microscope. Once I learned what the word meant I fancied myself a naturalist, and took great pleasure in the observations I made in the woods and marsh near our home. My favorite childhood books were Hugh Lofting's *Doctor Dolittle* series and Daniel Defoe's *Robinson Crusoe*. Later I read about Charles Darwin and John J. Audubon.

In high school I excelled in science subjects and was placed in advanced courses; I also concentrated on English and foreign languages. There was time for playing on the soccer team, practicing the cello, and writing for the school and community newspapers. I became more aware of chronic social problems, and passionately so. I took the AP courses in history and studied the evolution of man's endeavors to solve those problems. I discovered distinctions between various interpretations of objective history and visions of the future. I realized that while advances in technology were necessary for progress, their proper application was an equally important and complex issue. Technical advances in medicine, for example, are in themselves amazing but their utility is subject to ethical and economic considerations.

I viewed college as an opportunity for experimentation as well as for the pursuit of my established interests. I became interested in health care specifically while volunteering in the local Cerebral Palsy clinic. Our group worked primarily with young people in a weekly swim/gym program. I met on a regular basis with two boys who shared an uneasy friendship and were eager for attention from an adult. Once established, our relationship was a source of pleasure for me as well as for them. Hospital work in later years confirmed my positive attitude towards dealing with sick and handicapped people. Though I took premedical courses at Williams College, I was not intensely career-oriented. I wanted a broad education and chose history as its foundation. For my junior year I sought an experience outside the "ivory tower" of Williams. I attended the London School of Economics & Political Science, whose highly specialized curriculum complemented my more diverse program at home. Stimulated by the emphasis on independent work, I immersed myself in the study of modern history.

Following graduation from Williams I received a grant to serve as field assistant with a research team studying the physiology of the Black Rhinoceros in Kenya under the auspices of Harvard and Nairobi Universities. We worked with the Kenyan Game Dept. in moving the rare animals from highly poached areas to safer ones. Our group had access to the temporarily captive rhinos in order to record physiological data relevant to thermoregulation studies.

When the rhino project ended, I stayed in Kenya to work with an ecologist doing a study of the carrying capacity for elephants in Meru National Park. When herds are confined to limited areas, their feeding destroys the vegetation quickly, and an aspect of large game management is determining the population a park can support. For a rapidly growing nation like Kenya, the problem is real; people are hungry and have little sympathy for animals that leave the parks to eat their crops. Actually I found the human side of the issue to be crucial; as both our needs and technology grow, so does our potential environmental impact. Development programs including a rational allocation of resources have become necessary to provide for both the "manmade" and "natural" worlds.

Medical care is one especially important part of the development strategy I'm referring to and is the focus of my interest. All through Kenya, Sudan, and Egypt I was amazed at the success of medical clinics that have, in fighting infectious disease, helped to raise birth and survival rates and life expectancies—but not necessarily the quality of life! More children survive into adulthood only to suffer from chronic malnutrition. Yet impoverished parents often rely on their children for security and disregard government urging to limit family size. I feel that lay health education is an important adjunct to medical care programs.

The two years I spent in Africa and the Middle East experiencing vastly different cultures and living conditions have given me a new perspective here at home. I also gained confidence from dealing with accidents and other difficult situations that I hadn't encountered in school. I feel strongly that I have the potential for personal as well as professional growth in the study and practice of medicine.

E s s a y   # 4

At the age of six I started studying insects under my magnifying glass and by the time I was ten, I had already detonated my first explosive with the help of a Mr. Wizard chemistry kit. These are just the first entries in my scientific resume. In high school I became more serious, studying the areas of electronics and meteorology at the Talcott Mountain Science Center in Avon, Connecticut, and holographic photography at the Weizmann Institute of Science in Israel. Once in college, I became a biology teaching assistant and a physics tutor in addition to my regular schedule of science courses. There was rarely a time when I was not involved in some type of science-related activity. More recently, however, I have discovered that there is another world outside the scientific establishment: one that has made me aware of my inner strengths, my capacity to handle responsibility, and my sensitivity towards other people.

It was in the mountains of Wyoming where I learned the true meaning of challenge. As part of a two-week winter camping and survival course taught by the National Outdoor Leadership School (NOLS), I camped out in temperatures of twenty-seven degrees below zero, cross-country skied with a seventy pound pack, and climbed to altitudes that could not sustain vegetation. Survival, not the allurement of the alpine environment, was my only thought. It was not until I had time to reflect upon my adventures that I realized what it meant to persevere. I knew I could apply those characteristics of determination, will, and desire to any future situation.

My participation in an American Youth Hostel (AYH) leadership training course is where I learned the skills of leadership and responsibility. Here, for the first time, I was responsible for the welfare of others as I conducted a group bicycle tour across Ohio. After nine days of pedaling through the farmlands of Pandora, replacing the broken spokes of Fuji bicycles and settling the common arguments among my companion bikers, i.e., when to eat, whose turn it was to clean up, and how to spend group funds, I understood what responsibility entailed. It was more than directing a group towards a destination. It was listening to their problems and helping each one see different viewpoints. It was consoling a forty five-year-old woman when her rear wheel was hopelessly bent, and it was helping a fellow college student whip up a late dinner for an unruly group.

While the NOLS and AYH programs are just two short experiences in my life, what I took from them has enabled me to see how important people are in my future. I know now that I enjoy working with all types of people, that I will not shy away from difficult problems, and that I have the skills and temperament to handle various situations. This knowledge, coupled with my interest in science, has inspired me to seek a career that combines humanism with scientific expertise.

This summer I have accepted a position in the Hartford Hospital Student Fellowship Program where I am involved in pulmonary function testing under the supervision of Dr. Arthur DeGraff. This program has enabled me to witness certain clinical procedures which have confirmed what I always felt inherent in the medical profession: that physicians are not just scientists but have a concern for other people, are able to persevere in difficult situations, and accept responsibility in life and death matters. While there is a great physical difference between the mountains of Wyoming and the corridors of Hartford Hospital, both have given me a new insight into myself and the medical profession. I now hope to study medicine and become the type of physician who is as comfortable with a stethoscope as he is with a patient's complaint.

Essay # 5

I would like to share a number of personal experiences that contributed to my decision to become a physician.

I first became interested in science in high school when an extremely talented teacher introduced me to the study of biology. Although the course was only an introductory one, this teacher went far beyond the standard curriculum. Not only did the class dissect frogs, grasshoppers, and worms, but it also proceeded under his direction to dissect cow eyes, and the brains and hearts of sheep. As the course progressed, the teacher's enthusiasm for his subject made me, in turn, eager to learn more. Thus my introduction to science at the high school level was very positive, and I looked forward to pursuing a science related career.

Another high school experience was also to prove instrumental in my future career choice. I was involved in a program in which students volunteered at Suffolk Development Center, a state-run mental institution in Melville, New York. Each volunteer was assigned to one patient on a regular basis. My charge, Joey, was a nineteen-year-old boy, who was blind, mentally retarded, and crippled. Quite frankly, the experience at first made me uncomfortable—I had never before been exposed to such severely handicapped people—but my initial feeling subsided as I became more involved with helping Joey perform simple tasks which, for him, were major accomplishments. This experience made me sensitive to the need to provide facilities for those whose health is mentally or physically impaired, and taught me that patience, care, and determination are needed to help such people. It was at this time that I began to focus on a career in medicine.

Because I was aware that the practice of medicine involved not only scientific principles, but a real understanding of the human condition, I sought in college to place my interest in science within a broad humanist perspective. I particularly enjoyed my Classics courses, and as for my science courses, it was Electron Microscopy that made the deepest impression on me. Here I was able to view in fine detail the complexity of cells and tissues. This course also provided me with an opportunity to work independently—preparing tissue, examining it under the microscope, and analyzing the various histological structures.

During my college years, I was able to observe the practical application of scientific knowledge. For example, I spent the month of January of my sophomore year in the Human Genetics Department of the

Yale University School of Medicine. I attended medical school genetics classes, as well as various medical conferences. Most important, however, under the direction of Dr. Xandra O. Breakfield, I engaged in an independent research project involving the bloodstream activity of the enzyme dopamine-B-hydroxylase and its possible basis of genetic inheritance. Although the results of the project were inconclusive, the experience proved to be very helpful to me, because it gave me an understanding of how scientific research can be used to study clinical problems.

My understanding of the field of medicine was enhanced during the following summer when, as a student intern, I was able to observe the activities of physicians in various specialties at Booth Memorial Hospital in Flushing, New York. These specialties included General Surgery, Pathology, Pediatrics, Endocrinology, and Radiology. I also spent time in the Emergency Room, the Clinic, and the Intensive Care Unit. This experience enabled me to appreciate the role of the doctor in both a hospital setting and private practice. In addition, my internship gave me an introduction to the advanced technology used in modern hospitals, and it also allowed me to observe firsthand the more intangible components of the practice of the art of medicine: the care, compassion, and dedication that these professionals demonstrated.

Because my experience at Booth was so valuable, I wanted to use the next summer to add to my knowledge of the medical field. I applied, therefore, to the Sarah Lawrence Program for Pre-Medical Students at Lawrence Hospital in Bronxville, New York, and I have been accepted. This program attempts to provide an overview of the medical experience while focusing on the students' personal interests. I look forward, in particular, to spending time in Emergency Medicine, Endocrinology, and Pathology.

My various experiences in high school and college have shown me that the field of medicine demands intelligence, integrity, compassion, and commitment, and I believe that my personal attributes will enable me to make a positive contribution to the profession.

E s s a y   # 6

···

*T*hroughout my young life, I have constantly strived to answer the questions presented before me. Some have been easy—"What is the square root of 9,801?" (99). Others have not been quite so simple—"What do you want to be when you grow up? Why?" My first science courses in the 7th grade stimulated my interest in the medical profession. Before long, I had even selected a specialty: neurosurgery.

Although I have almost always had set goals, I have not been afraid to challenge them. From my sophomore year through my high school graduation, I worked as a typist/computer programmer (15-20 hr/wk, five d/wk) in a small music stand business. This job not only allowed me to improve my dexterity, but also to contribute to my family's strained budget; thus I tasted my first responsibility in the real world. Although I briefly considered a career in computers, I soon realized that I would gain little sense of contribution to other people.

During my first two years in college I worked as an attendant (20 hr/wk) at a local video arcade. Constant interaction with customers made my employment there well worthwhile. The summer following my sophomore year, I found a job as a lab assistant (30 hr/wk, 1 1/2 mos) in the neuroresearch center of the VA Hospital in Palo Alto, CA. At first I worked as a simple lab technician. Before long, however, my supervisor became convinced that I had the potential to do more, and I was taught to inject rats and to perform a simple surgical maneuver—crush a nerve in the leg and sew the surrounding muscles and skin back together. Although I worked in this lab for a relatively short time, the exposure piqued my interest in the field of research, an option I am currently considering quite seriously.

Acting on this new-found interest in research, I took on a job in the psychobiology labs on Berkeley campus (10-15 hrs/wk, 5 d/wk 1st sem; 5 h/wk, 3 d/wk 2nd and 3rd sems, as projects became less demanding). I wrote two reports while receiving academic credit, describing how a component of long-term memory in rats could be affected by certain drugs. In these papers I designed several original statistical analyses and, in a recently published paper of which I was a coauthor, we showed for the first time that long-term memory could be used in a manner not previously considered. Here I was able to interact with professionals as I gained a much more in-depth, rewarding exposure to life in the labs.

In addition to volunteering my time in the labs, I have supported myself by typing an organic chemistry textbook (10-20 h/wk, 5 d/wk; full-time during the summers). This job has been particularly rewarding, as the author allowed me to start editing the book from a student's point of view. My goal has been to present organic chemistry to future students in a clearer and more interesting fashion than it was presented to me.

Although I have enjoyed the challenge of medical research and studies, I have gained increasing satisfaction from contributing my services to others. For the past three years, I have participated in our campus "Buddy" orientation program. Perhaps my greatest satisfaction came when one particular "buddy" (who had been out of school for almost eight years) came to me for help. At first, the shock of university life seemed to be pushing her on the verge of a nervous breakdown, but as I continued to volunteer countless hours of both tutoring (something I have always enjoyed doing) and moral support, she finally began to calm down, and now performs at or near the top of her classes. There may be nothing on this earth more rewarding than helping someone else realize his or her potential!

Having repeatedly reaffirmed my career choice as a physician and/or medical researcher, I realized that I had virtually no experience helping actual patients. Consequently, I started working this February in the ever busy trauma center at San Francisco General. Before long I found myself working every Friday night from 11 p.m. to 4 a.m., helping physicians and nurses complete a variety of tasks (lab runs, gurney sheet-changes, etc.). More important, however, my primary role has been to provide moral support to and respond to the needs of often-confused and frightened patients. I have even been able to use my Spanish-speaking ability (acquired in part from my Mexican-American background) to help patients that did not know English. Trauma room life has been so exciting that I constantly find myself watching the physicians at work and helping them in any way possible, even by performing CPR on occasion. The satisfaction I have received in making the patients' visits as pleasant as possible, as well as in making the staff's work a little easier, has been inestimable. At four in the morning, I'm almost never ready to leave!

My biggest question now is no longer whether I want to be a doctor, but whether I want to be a specialist, as earlier planned, or a GP, where my services could be more useful, especially in needy Latin American countries. The decision may not be too difficult if my experiences keep going the way they have been!

*T*he problems of our society, particularly those related to health care delivery, are numerous. Solutions to these problems will arise from individuals who have a broad view of society and the will to contribute their talents to society. I feel that I possess these qualities and can best contribute my talents to society as a physician.

It was as a junior in high school that I began to consider pursuing a career in medicine. I decided to participate in Project SOAR, a summer premedical program at Xavier. As a participant in Project SOAR, I had the opportunity to learn about medicine by speaking to students who had been accepted by medical schools. By exposing me to college-level work and successful premedical students, whose academic backgrounds were similar to my own, SOAR enhanced my confidence in my academic ability and encouraged me to pursue a career in medicine.

During my senior year in high school, I enrolled as a part-time student in the Concurrent Admissions program at Xavier, where I attended six semester hours of credit. My experiences in Project SOAR and in the Concurrent Admissions program influenced my decision to matriculate at Xavier, full-time, as a chemistry major.

Pursuing a career in medicine is a challenge that should be undertaken only by persons who have a genuine interest in health care. I have learned that I would enjoy working as a physician to improve the quality of health care in our society. My experience in the United Negro College Fund Summer Premedical Institute affirmed my interest in medicine and provided me with information about a variety of exciting medical careers. I will participate in the Summer Research Fellowship Program at the Cornell University Medical College, where my research assignment will involve nuclear medicine. Clinical exposure is also a component of the program. I look forward to the experience, since it should provide me with a better understanding of the role of research in medicine.

At Xavier I have had the opportunity to gain teaching experience. I instructed a general chemistry class, one day each week, during the fall semester, and I taught high school students who participated in a summer chemistry program. Assisting my students in reaching their academic goals was very rewarding. Teaching was very enjoyable, because it allowed me to work with people in a meaningful way. I feel that I would enjoy practicing medicine, since it would allow me to interact with people in a similar manner.

Presently I am interested in diagnostic imaging and academic medicine. Because I am very interested in social issues, I am also considering pursuing the degree of Master of Public Health, so that I may better serve the health care delivery system.

Physicians, like other citizens, have a vested interest in the well being of society. They should be involved not only in treating patients, but also in solving the problems of health care delivery, such as providing medical care to the indigent and the elderly. Although my career goals are not definite at this time, I feel that my background is such that I can pursue a career in any area of medicine and make a meaningful contribution to society. Moreover, my ability to work with others strengthens my conviction that medicine is my vocation. For these reasons, I believe that I can best serve society as a physician.

E s s a y   # 8

D uring college my closest friends and I have spent hours analyzing our personalities and determining what makes us unique. We explored what motivated our becoming good doctors and why it would make us happy, and we examined the underlying currents which influence and motivate our thoughts and actions. For me, the most visible current is communication: being able to articulate my thoughts, being able to make others experience them, being receptive to the ideas of others, and being understanding.

As a poet, I feel that in order to write meaningful poetry, one must have a clear sense of how to communicate effectively. Whenever I begin a poem, I remember the advice of my high school English teacher: "a poem should be wordless, as the flight of birds." By choosing precise words, by paying attention to the sounds of phrases sewn together, and by evoking clear images, a poem is created. It should grip and move the reader immediately just as a person, seeing a perfectly wedged V-line of Canadian geese flying overhead toward the horizon, stops, catches his breath, and reflects on the beauty that has passed. It is through poetry that I try to recapture my feelings during those wordless moments, and I try to pass them on to the reader.

My need to be a communicator extends beyond poetry. Learning foreign languages, peer counseling, student advising, tutoring, and acting are activities in which I have participated. Each activity emphasizes a particular discipline of communication. Learning foreign languages stems from my enjoyment of communicating with people of different cultures in their native languages. By speaking a language common to us both, communication barriers are bridged. A peer counseling center offers students a comfortable place to talk. By attentive listening, the counselor helps the student clarify his thoughts and feelings and explore options to his problems. Student advisors form quick, friendly rapport with the incoming freshmen. Throughout the year, the advisors offer guidance and suggest options and opportunities at college by relating their own experiences. The tutoring process centers on imparting knowledge. The tutor must motivate the student to cope with his difficulties, to overcome them, and to finally enjoy learning the subject. My involvement in acting and directing is a form of personal expression through interpretation. I draw upon my experiences and intuition to present realistic, complex portrayals.

Through foreign languages, peer counseling, student advising, tutoring, and theater, I have explored and developed my communicative abilities. It is this aspect of my personality that will be challenged by a medical career. Whenever one studies foreign languages, one learns to be receptive to a foreign culture. With a perceptive and sympathetic ear is how the peer counselor listens. A student advisor is a freshman's first friend, and a tutor becomes a trusted teacher. An actor or a director investigates the endless possibilities of presenting characters and scenes in certain viewpoints. A doctor embodies the essential characteristics of all these people. A receptive student, a patient listener, an approachable friend, an informative conveyor, and a perceptive examiner are the types of communicator a doctor must be at all times. Recognizing this, I have made a concerted effort to extend and to nurture my capacity for expressing my thoughts, making others experience them, and hearing out the thoughts and ideas of others.

"J ohn, put another log on the fire." Sparks flew into the night sky. Only the front of me was warm. It was always like that—your back was always cold.

"You still want to be a doctor?"

I nodded.

"In this country you have to be the best. It's the hardest anywhere."

"Then I'll be the best."

"You must rely on yourself. I help as much as is possible, but here only the top get scholarship. In Poland it's easier, but here only a few get the whole shot. I think you can do it if you work hard."

"You know how I work when I want something."

"Yes, I know. Just take a day at a time and you'll do OK."

My father sipped his beer. Silence fell as we watched the flames dance on the logs.

As a young boy I would always look forward to camping with my father. Talk would fly over hundreds of topics as we walked through the forest or sat around the fire at night. He would ramble on about everything from his high blood pressure to nuclear reactions in the sun. Most of the time I never really understood all of what he said, yet I became charmed by the ideas and thrilled when he would tell me something new. I wanted to know everything, but the more that I knew, the more I realized that I didn't know. Occasionally, I found this to be true too late, as unintentional explosions from my lab in the garage resulted in severe reprimands from my parents.

With age came moderation and a more formal road to education. The innocence of childhood tinkering had matured into the seriousness of adult tinkering, and with it the expectations I had of myself. Although my meager laboratory of childhood was no more, my love for the unknown was alive and well. In the real world though, things seldom went as smoothly as they had in the past.

"I can't get this experiment to work!" I would assert to myself while sitting at my lab bench. "Two o'clock in the morning and two weeks gone by. I swear I'll see these petri-dishes in my sleep. Dr. Youderian always said, 'This is what it's all about.' Indeed, perhaps this time…"

Those experiences when things didn't work were just as invaluable as those experiences when things did. After getting to know and appreciate the work and dedication required to discern even the smallest amount of information, it became clear to me why learning in the health sciences is truly lifelong.

Then there were those things which I found one learned only by doing. As a volunteer, I remember one night a young man my age came in with a knife wound to the chest.

"The lung is collapsed," the physician said. There was no time to anesthetize. Five people and myself held the patient down. As the physician made the incision, the boy writhed in pain. The screams made the hair on your neck stand up. As the blood spilled out onto the floor, you could see others around grimace and turn away.

"Look at that guy," I said to my friend nearby in a motion that indicated I was talking about the doctor. "Cool as a cucumber. Just another night at California Hospital for him."

I realized then that there was a lot more to medicine than getting an "A" in a class. I also realized that I still had a long way to go.

For now, that journey is really only beginning. I've taken "a day at a time," and as my father said years ago, I've done OK. I've worked and planned for a long time, and it's gratifying, as well as slightly frightening, to see it all culminating so quickly now. During those years I hope I've grown and learned such that I might begin a career in medicine. I don't think I ever have been, or ever will be, the "best," but I do know that I've never stopped trying.

E s s a y   # 1 0

A s the midnight moon rose to illuminate the smooth rock face, I checked the knot of the last camper's climbing harness and glanced at our tents more than 1000 feet below. Preparing for our final descent, we were exhausted and six hours overdue. I focused on guiding each novice through her first rappel: Brain and hands coordinated to guarantee safety, while voice and touch offered reassurance. From the mountainside I will bring these skills of intellectual alertness, individualized care and attention to detail to my patients' bedsides.

My interest in medicine, fueled by diverse academic and extra-curricular experiences, is ultimately rooted in my desire to empower others while attending to their physical and psychological needs. In both health care and climbing, positions of knowledge require one to enable others to care for themselves. Had I not insisted the campers learn the knots and work as a team, our forced rappel could easily have proved disastrous.

My approach to teaching mirrors my conception of medicine: continual hands-on learning backed by solid science and the empower-ment of both provider and patient. Summoned to a "terrible accident," my wilderness first aid students hurry to care for their "injured" class-mates sprawled on the grass. Applying new knowledge, these future providers discover their powers of analysis by examining patients and their creativity by building such things as a traction splints from ban-dannas, a stick and a shoe. I share my enthusiasm for medicine by allowing students to experience it as a lifelong learning process requiring ingenuity and self-motivation.

When weather and geography seal off modern medicine, wilderness first aid approaches doctoring. Trapped on an exposed ridge by dark-ness and a June snow storm, I duct-taped a plastic tarp around the sleeping bag of a hypothermic backpacker, improvising a "hypowrap." In the absence of a thermometer, I could only gauge the effects of treatment by asking, "Josh, if you were driving from Alaska to Baja, where would you be?" That night, my wilderness first aid training, my compassion and my analytical abilities converged to save a life.

Invigorated by the practice of medicine, I am even more rewarded when former students describe how they prevented and treated back

100

country injuries. My EMT course and experiences as a back-country first aid provider and as a first aid teacher motivate me to make a career in medicine, deepening and broadening my skills. As a doctor, my work will have an even greater effect.

My extensive work on issues of violence further testifies to my commitment to empowering others. Providing practical assistance as a restraining order court advocate, I am educated by those I serve. My undergraduate senior thesis found inspiration in a 20 year-old African American woman's fight to maintain her dignity in an unjust world. Burdened by inflexible welfare and day-care systems, this woman desperately wanted her high school diploma; it offered more independence than any restraining order. Trapped, she returned to her abusive ex boyfriend because she needed a baby-sitter for their children during school hours. This woman's alarming situation motivated me to investigate the impact of domestic violence upon economic well-being. Inspired by methods of scientific research, I turned my queries into a rigorous econometric thesis, providing a forum for academic, personal and social interests.

Academic introspection on violence also finds expression as active caring through RESPONSE, a counseling hot-line for victims of violence. One caller, a nine-year-old girl struggling to describe abuses beyond her vocabulary, drew from me, "You are a brave girl." She paused and whispered, "No one has ever told me that." This moment of connection restored a bit of human dignity, for both of us. I never talked to her again, yet her memory motivates me to continually reach out.

Shadowing a gynecologist at Johns Hopkins I realized how the artful combination of surgical skill and sensitive questions allows treatment of the whole person rather than just a child's painful genital growth. Inspired by this doctor's ability to draw upon both technical and personal skills to address an array of medical and life issues, I married teaching skills with therapy-driven techniques for remedial classes at a youth psychiatric hospital program. Directly involved in shaping patient therapy programs, I learned of the inextricability of these two seemingly distinct facets of well-being: education and psychiatric health.

Supported by the Rockefeller Traveling Fellowship over the coming year, I again unite technical and personal skills to address health and social issues: I will establish a first aid teaching program in a South African township. The dire health care needs of these townships are complicated by poverty, violence and the clash between traditional and modern medicine. Adapting wilderness medicine to third world conditions, I will teach community members to teach, ensuring empowerment and the integration of local issues. To this year of challenge and exploration, I bring my energy and creativity. I will carry back a refined sense of self and a deeper understanding of medicine's role in society.

E s s a y   # 1 1

I spent my junior year of college at Queens' College, Cambridge University in England. There I studied chemistry and biochemistry (i.e. natural sciences). Credit for my course work in England is to be applied toward my Cornell University B.A. degree. As of July 14, the final credit that I will receive for this work does not appear on my official transcript. Also, since I was abroad, I was not able to discuss with my faculty advisor which courses I should take during my senior year. Therefore, my academic record in this application is incomplete. I will notify AMCAS of corrections as soon as possible.

Summer activities:

19XX—Volunteer at Pascack Valley Hospital Department of Radiology (Westwood, NJ). Helped with patients, aided x-ray and computer tomography technicians, ran errands for department supervisors.

19XX—Lab technician at Rockefeller University (New York City). Conducted synthesis and purification of a protein tumor growth factor (co-researcher of paper pending publication).

19XX—Continued research at Rockefeller University. Synthesized and examined analogs of tumor growth factor to discern relationship between structure and activity.

(Editor's note: The dates in this essay have been obscured to protect the writer's anonymity.)

Essay #12

W hile exploring a wide range of activities, I discovered an increasing interest in the medical profession. Although desiring a general background, I felt drawn to this field by the challenge and opportunity to employ a variety of my skills and interests in benefitting others in an area of critical need. My love of animals and desire to help the rural worker originally drew me to veterinary medicine and the animal science major. However, after a year of college and exposure to rural areas lacking proper health care, I realized that a greater need existed for physicians.

Exposed to medicine early in life through my mother, a lab technician, and a brother, a doctor, I developed a natural curiosity that led from visits to my mother's lab to volunteering and later working in Clinical Pathology at Upstate. I rotated through the labs performing routine lab tests and became one of the few workers proficient in troubleshooting the equipment. To increase my contact with patients, I requested work as a morning blood-drawer and volunteered in the E.R. The time spent listening to and comforting the patients, especially the elderly, was invaluable.

At college, after performing RIA's for a year in an endocrinology research lab, I resolved to develop a safer assay. The next year was spent researching the alternate methods and finding professors interested in supporting my project. The ELISA method for progesterone in dogs I developed as an undergraduate research project then expanded into my honor's thesis.

Wanting to develop my other interests as well as pursue my goal to become a rural physician, I chose to continue with animal science, a flexible program offering many of the medically oriented courses. I developed a program strong in genetics and statistics while taking electives in the humanities and computers.

Through travel, reading, work, and various organizations, I pursued my other interests. My work as a computer teaching assistant and terminal operator this year will supplement my programming minor. To act on issues important to me, I joined AgPac, the Curriculum committee, and the campaign committees. Interested in international affairs, I was fortunate to be an Orientation Counselor to the entire International Living Center for foreign students. Enjoying the role of an O.C., I became a student advisor to 12 students, a position with similar but more lasting and personal responsibilities. To further improve my teaching skills, I offered my services as a tutor through Ho-Nun-De-Kah and worked as a genetics teaching assistant responsible for a 30 student lab section. Riding since high school, I competed throughout the Northeast on the Cornell Riding Team and qualified for Regionals. My continuing interest in horses expanded into organizing horse shows, organizing public service symposiums, and teaching the handicapped to ride. My painting, drawing, and violin playing found an outlet through the various club activities.

These interests remained secondary to and contributed to a growing interest in the social problems facing rural areas. A summer working and living with a farm family and the many conversations we had concerning the difficulties of rural life, confirmed my desire to assist the rural community. At present I work for the Fresh Air Fund Camp which introduces innercity NYC poor and handicapped children to a healthy rural atmosphere while promoting respect for the farmer's role.

Farmers work 80-hour weeks in a high-risk job without the benefit of retirement plans, medical plans, paid vacations, or paid sick days. Due to a low population density and thus political invisibility, rural areas frequently suffer from inadequate health care as they are unable to receive even the government support the urban poor receive. In addition, the long hours, understaffing, lack of modern facilities, and isolation in rural practices discourage many physicians.

Aware of these difficulties, I am committed to operating a clinic as a family practitioner, utilizing an effective support staff similar in organization to the Frontier Nursing Service. This practice allows the physicians to use their time more effectively in giving quality and humanistic care. It is my hope to establish such a clinic in a rural area presently lacking in health care.

Essay #13

Two roads diverged in a wood, and I —
I took the one less traveled by,
And that has made all the difference

T he close of Robert Frost's poem perfectly captures the image of how I ultimately decided to become a physician. As I look back on this decision, a clear path emerges leading to this new course in life. That wandering road, no matter how it meandered, always stressed both my humanitarian and scientific interests in the medical profession.

Even when peering back into my earliest recollections as a child, I see the beginnings of my decision to become a doctor. I remember fondly many nights spent sitting on my grandfather's lap after his heart surgery, trying my best to emulate the actions of the doctors and nurses that had saved his life. After every mock procedure I performed, I would ask him loudly, "Feel better?" His one-word reply was always, "Yes." Still I stood with a sense of incredulity and awe as the technological machinery hummed next to my grandfather's bedside. Even then, the scientific complexity of the profession intrigued me.

My lifelong interest in the sciences was fueled by my father. When I was a boy, he would always make sure there was a chemistry set, a book on electronics, or a brand new microscope under the tree at Christmas; however, this exploration of new technology was always tempered with a humanitarian element provided mostly by my mother. Teaching by example, my mother was the person who was willing to help anyone. I saw as a child how in any crisis, from the death of a family friend to the random person without gas, my mother always supported the person in need. It would be events like these which would eventually forge my desire to cut a new course for myself, one devoid of unexpected bends in the road.

When I received the chance to return to school, I began by meticulously retaking all the classes I had withdrawn from in the past. This renewed dedication to education was sparked by a new goal, excellence. What started out as a desire to do my best in college turned instead into an aspiration to pursue a career which would fill my life with knowledge and enjoyment. After completing my courses at the Community College, my next responsibility entailed finding an undergraduate institution which would complement my interest in the unity between the humanities and the sciences. Austin College stood out as the perfect place, an almost mirror-image of everything I wanted a college to be. The supportive attitudes of my fellow students and the approachability of my professors confirmed my initial feelings and bolstered my confidence. As a result, I applied for and received the chance to do research at the University of Texas Health Science Center in San Antonio. Under the supervision of Dr. Christi Walter, I had the unique opportunity to witness and experience, for a short while, all the excitement and difficulties that face today's modern research scientist. It was my job to develop a new protocol for the laboratory. At the end of the month when I saw the creatine phosphokinase assay I developed from scientific articles had actually worked, I could not contain my excitement. This positive experience, coupled with the following semester's systemic physiology class, led me to apply for summer research fellowships. Months later, I returned to the University of Texas Health Science Center to work in the physiology department. Currently, I am studying how varying concentrations of estrogen effect the Cytomeglavirus expression rate and a bovine carotid artery cell line in the laboratory of Dr. Mark Steinhelper. I hope to publish an abstract and contribute to a paper using the data I am generating.

All throughout my life the search for knowledge has been connected with the desire to help others. In a clinical setting, my reasons for wanting to be a physician were solidified every day I walked into Parkland Memorial Hospital, Children's Medical Center, or the Methodist Hospital in San Antonio. At each of these hospitals, I witnessed differently how the love of humanity I had learned as a child merged with the scientific aspects of medicine. Assisting in the organ donation program at Parkland provided testimony to the important and sometimes difficult decision of giving life to another by simply offering one's organs. At Children's Medical Center I attended and entertained sick children, reaffirming my belief that quality tine spent with a patient can greatly improve the healing process. Now, at Methodist Hospital in San Antonio, I am working in the emergency room in order to glimpse the many differences between public university hospitals and private ones.

I am so lucky to have a second chance at spending my life doing something I love. I feel that through the vehicle of research, I will be allowed to define how medicine is practiced in the future. Coupled with teaching, I hope to have the opportunity to shape the careers of future physicians. Blending clinical medicine, instruction, and research, I desire to make a lasting contribution to the medical field. During my arduous journey, numerous people have contributed to the person I have become. As a physician, I want to return some of the innate goodness that has been showered upon me by others. Great physicians must have confidence, intelligence, a sense of humor and impart a feeling of trust to their patients; however, boiled down to its simplest elements, medicine has as its base two facets: an almost purely scientific contribution and a more elusive humanitarian element. Although not always by conscious effort until recently, I have strived to develop both of these throughout my life. Two paths did emerge in the woods, and I took the path less traveled. Forging my own road, I paused to blend the best of these two sides, the humanitarian and the scientific, until they became one. When the path emerged, I grabbed the opportunity and feel I have made the most of my choice. Now I pause, waiting expectantly for the signal allowing me to continue my journey to its ultimate destination; that of becoming a physician.

Essay #14

....

T o work with people, to help them when they are sick, and to find ways to prevent illnesses is a challenge. When I volunteered at the Virginia Home for the Disabled in Richmond, I often felt that many illnesses were preventable. I also had the opportunity to help my father treat patients, and I was always thrilled by the successful administration of medicine.

Academic preparation for medical school initially dominated my school career at the University of Richmond. However, in the last year I, under the tutelage of a professor at the University of Richmond, found myself very involved in a research program which resulted in the publication of a paper. This program taught me how to maintain endurance and interest in an academic area and was therefore the most educational experience in my college career. My communicative and persuasive skills were also developed, for the research involved the competitive procurement of grants as well as the lecturing to audiences of varying backgrounds on the subject matter.

As a result of the emphasis on the research project, I did not take all of the courses required for premedical preparation, but I had an unexpected opportunity to compensate the following year. My original plan was to join the Peace Corps between college and medical school. I succeeded in graduating (cum laude) early. Unfortunately the assignment was delayed for more than a year. It was during this time that I continued to carry on my interest in research. I worked as a laboratory technician and as an assistant in an OB-GYN practice. As a technician in a private laboratory in Massachusetts, I was able to perform supervised experiments in order to identify and isolate clotting factors in Horseshoe crab blood— with possible implications of medicinal value.

Upon moving to Virginia, I began a part-time occupation in an OB GYN practice. Working in a medical practice has made me realize that the need for communicating information is just as vital as learning it. Therefore, I have tried to prepare myself in this area as well. Being raised in a bilingual (American/German) household, I am at ease in speaking either language. I added Spanish during my first year in college at St. Louis University in Madrid, Spain. Further, being somewhat of a history buff has allowed me to extend my communicative skills as well: I am currently an active docent for the Fairfax County Park Authority, and thus I give tours at a representative Virginia plantation named Sully.

To some extent travel allowed me insight into the culture, religion, and needs of other people. In addition, another very enlightening experience occurred during a recent summer in Woods Hole, Massachusetts. I partook in a marine research program given by Boston University and was confronted with a vast new area of information in both historic and scientific respects. The summer courses centered on detailed studies and independent research projects dealing with the oceans and their inhabitants. Emphasis was also placed on the individual's ability to cooperate and to withstand the physical hardships that a small, crowded sailing vessel foisted upon one. My research project on this cruise resulted in a paper on the polychaete population in the Bay of Fundy.

My recreational hobbies include a wide variety of non-medically oriented activities. For example, I am learning how to play the classical guitar. I maintain a productive herb and flower garden. I enjoy windsurfing in the local waters. During the winter months, I also spend a great deal of time involved in ice-skating, skiing, wood-carving, and needlecraft. Furthermore, I sew most of my wardrobe. I have been involved with jewelry-making, with mechanical car repairs, and with the German School Choir. I also learned some veterinary medicine when my entire family took a summer course at Cornell University Adult Education.

My life has been exciting and diversified. Even so, I have never lost sight of the quest to become a physician.

E s s a y # 1 5

·······································

*M*y interest in medicine is rooted in various medically related positions I have held in clinical and research settings. I was awarded an NIH summer fellowship at Roswell Park Memorial Institute, Buffalo, New York, where I characterized an anti-leukemia-lymphoma monoclonal antibody. This work won the institute's Sydney Farber Award for Outstanding Independent Research. Conducting research in a laboratory associated with several hospitals offered insights into the relationship between basic science and health care. The following summer I worked as a dissector for the Department of Anatomy, State University of New York at Buffalo Medical School, preparing prosections for the gross anatomy course. I enjoyed both the analytical approach of laboratory research and the precision of dissection: hence I sought further experience in the biomedical field.

During my freshman year at Cornell I applied to the College Scholar Program as a means of combining interests in the biological and social sciences. Under the auspices of this program, competitively selected undergraduates design their own majors, integrating broad topics not accommodated by the usual curriculum. I am pursuing concentrations in cell biology and Soviet studies.

One summer I worked as an emergency room volunteer at the Buffalo General Hospital. At the same time, as a Summer Research Fellow at the Department of Oral Biology, State University of New York at Buffalo Dental School, I prepared monoclonal antibodies against the oral pathogen Actinobacillus actinomycetemcomitans. These antibodies have since been patented by the university. This intensive, simultaneous exposure to biomedical research and clinical practice firmly established my resolve to pursue a career in medicine. It also persuaded me of the importance of research as a foundation underlying medical practice; consequently I have used the flexibility of the College Scholar Program to integrate research into my academic work. I substituted an independent research project of characterizing an Apium graviolens enzyme, in the course of which I used most basic biochemical techniques, for the traditional biochemistry lab course. Upon completion of this project I began research on the structure and function of glucose-6-phosphatase in conjunction with work being performed in the laboratory of Dr. William Arion, Department of Biochemistry, Molecular and Cell Biology, Cornell University.

Currently I am participating in the DeBakey Summer Program at the Department of Surgery, Baylor College of Medicine. I assist in cardiovascular surgery under Dr. E. Stanley Crawford at the Methodist Hospital of Houston, and work during my free time at the emergency room and trauma center of the nearby Benjamin Taub county hospital. Through this experience I have learned, by direct participation, aspects of the day to-day reality of cardiovascular surgery and trauma care; happily found myself capable of maintaining a first-year intern's hours; and, by working with patients in two so vastly different institutions, have been stimulated to reconsider some social aspects of the health care delivery system.

Essay #16

*M*y interest in becoming a physician has developed through exposure to both clinical medicine and investigative research. In the first area, I have had the opportunity to work in the office practice of an ophthalmologist and to observe surgery at three hospitals. In college, I successfully completed an Emergency Medical Technician training course. Throughout these experiences, I was impressed and inspired by the skill, dedication and compassion of the professionals with whom I worked and studied.

I was introduced to investigative medicine during an eight-week paid fellowship in the Tissue Typing Laboratory of the New York Blood Center. In this position I learned the basic histocompatibility tests necessary to match donors with recipients for kidney and bone marrow transplantation and studied the relationship between specific HLA factors and certain diseases such as Juvenile Macular Degeneration.

With a strong recommendation from the Blood Center, I procured a salaried position of greater scientific complexity and responsibility at Memorial Cancer Center. My extensive work in the immunohematology laboratory of Memorial has been the single most significant force in my decision to attend medical school.

The first summer I was responsible for establishment and maintenance of several of the first cell lines derived from patients with AIDS and the analysis of AIDS patients' immune response through measurement of lymphocyte transformation and Natural Killer Cell activity in vitro. I was the only student approved to work in the P-3, biological containment level, laboratory that year.

Our research was directed at determining the efficacy of several drugs in restoring AIDS patients' immune response. Although I was working with patient blood in a high-containment facility and had realistic concerns for the safety of myself and others working in the laboratory, I felt extremely fortunate to have the opportunity to use my recently acquired skills and to learn new procedures within a formal research design. My greatest satisfaction was observing the connection between what we were accomplishing in the laboratory and the plight of the AIDS patients with whom I met and talked.

During the following January, I returned to the immunohematology laboratory at Memorial where I was given the opportunity to continue with my work at a more sophisticated level and with more independence. My research during this month was aimed at determining whether the antigenic agent recognized when normal Natural Killer cells lyse AIDS target cells is similar to the antigen expressed by Epstein-Barr virus-infected cells.

This past summer I returned again to the laboratory to assist in supervising and was assigned to train new members of the team, one of whom was a doctor doing a fellowship in our laboratory. Strengthening the containment levels and adding additional precautions, I tested a newly proposed drug for AIDS, investigated the cell-mediated immunity of growth hormone-deficient patients, continued to maintain cell lines and learned a new interferon assay.

While I plan to defer my decision as to which field I will specialize in until after completion of my basic science studies, my experience at Memorial over the last two years has convinced me of my aptitude and interest in investigative research. However, in whatever field I choose, I will not divorce myself from patient care, for it was the personal interaction with patients that made my laboratory experience most meaningful.

Essay #17

My interests in biomedical science and the performing arts developed while I was a youngster. Fortunately, I have been able to enjoy both fields.

I have been working part-time during classes and full-time during breaks as a research technician at NIH, in Dr. John E. Folk's group (Natl. Inst. of Dental Research, Laboratory of Oral Biology and Physiology, Enzyme Chemistry Section). I assist Dr. Myung Hee Park. The focus of our work is one of the eukaryotic protein synthesis initiation factors, eIF-4D, a protein which contains the unusual amino acid hypusine (N -(4-amino-2 hydroxybutyl)lysine) as the result of post-translational modification: a lysine residue receives the butylamine portion of spermidine and is subsequently hydroxylated. The functions of the factor and its hypusine residue are unknown at this time. I was assigned my own project, the molecular cloning and sequencing of cDNA coding for eIF-4D. A bacteriophage lambda gt11 human hepatoma expression library was screened with oligonucleotide and antibody probes, and DNA sequencing experiments are currently underway. During the summer, I was engaged in the purification of eIF-4D from human erythrocytes by multistep chromatography and differential precipitation, analyzing the product by SDS-PAGE, LPLC and amino acid analysis. I am a coauthor of two papers and one abstract which describe that summer's work.

At George Mason University, I worked as research assistant to Prof. Suzanne Slayden of the Chemistry Department, studying the competition between protonolysis and rearrangement in certain trialkylboranes. In addition to learning the required air-sensitive techniques, I routinely analyzed the products using GC and proton NMR. I have been working with Dr. Slayden on a series of instructional videotapes designed to introduce various forms of spectroscopy to students of organic chemistry. These programs feature computer graphics and animations which I created in my spare time. One of them—"Interpreting NMR Spectra"—will be presented at the American Chemical Society's Mid-Atlantic Regional Meeting in Baltimore.

Prior to my return to college, I worked as a Senior Research Technician at the New York Blood Center, assisting Dr. Bernard Horowitz of the Blood Derivatives Program. Dr. Horowitz provided me with a working tutorial in experimental and process-scale protein chemistry, and eventually encouraged me to complete my formal education. My first year in his lab produced a chromatographic method for the purification of human leukocyte interferons. I characterized the material using isoelectric focusing, SDS-PAGE and 2D-PAGE, comparing the distribution of interferon subtypes in the highly purified chromatographic eluate to those in the non-recombinant interferon preparations then approved for use in human clinical trials. My efforts were then directed to the purification and characterization of human Factor VIII:C. Its association with von Willebrand factor was probed, and a number of RIAs and ELISAs were developed. The final phase of my work with Dr. Horowitz grew out of the AIDS epidemic: I investigated several methods of chemically inactivating viruses in blood products, aiming for conditions which were benign to Factor VIII procoagulant activity, yet left the injectables virus- and reagent-free. This project was passed on to other workers when I returned to school. I was a coauthor of two abstracts describing some of the interferon and Factor VIII work.

My laboratory experience also includes eighteen months as a clinical laboratory technician at Pathology Associates Laboratories in Beverly Hills, CA. I was responsible for running the daily "panel" of blood chemistries on an automated analyzer and flame photometer, and routinely performed RIAs and inoculated cultures. Other ongoing duties included the preparation of samples and the logging of patient information. I was initially hired as a courier by this lab, but was promoted into the laboratory at my request.

I have also been a performer (actor, singer and guitarist). I appeared in three Broadway shows, four national tours and numerous radio and television broadcasts. My association with the pathology lab started as one of the many jobs between shows, but proved to be the beginning of a new and more satisfying career, one free of the cyclic unemployment of the actor's life. My training in drama and music has proven to be a valuable asset in the biomedical field: an actor is taught to prepare and empathize; a musician develops manual dexterity and structured study habits; both must adapt to a wide variety of environments, and both require the ability to work in tandem with people of diverse backgrounds and interests.

Essay #18

Having been exposed to life in the medical profession at an early age, I have always considered a medical career as an option for my life. As a child, I looked at my father and saw only the respect with which he was treated and the wonderful financial compensations that his career provided at that time. These first impressions proved very tenacious, and it was only later that I began to realize that a physician's life is comprised of much more than wages and esteem.

My path to the medical profession has not been a straight one; although, it seemed as though it would be throughout my high school years. I never once doubted my desire to become a physician, and I sedulously worked to achieve my goal. It was during my third undergraduate year, however, that I began to contemplate the seriousness of my childhood decision. I realized that the main reason for my desire to become a physician was a direct result of exposure. I grew up in a family of health care providers, and I had never considered my own desires and passions. I began to explore history and English literature in my spare time, while I continued with my organic chemistry and my preparations for the MCAT. During this year, I began to seriously doubt my motivations, and I choose to study history as an alternative. I believe that this doubt has done more for my medical future than has the entire amount of time spent studying textbooks. After this year, I regained my desire to become a physician, but this time it was truly my desire and not one assumed from my surroundings. Several things had changed for me, however, and I set some goals for myself to complete before entering medical school.

My first goal was to spend at least a year in Latin America with a service organization, and I was given the opportunity to pursue this goal four months after graduation. I spent the better half of two years working in Guatemala with a medical/physical missions organization named HELPS International. It is a nonprofit organization that works in the northern mountains of Guatemala. I became the assistant to the Guatemalan director of HELPS International, and helped organize medical groups and construction teams from the United States. My job, as in any small organization, encompassed a wide variety of tasks that spanned all the way from guiding groups through the mountains to carrying water. I conducted public relations with the surrounding community, led away teams of medical personnel, helped translate in the medical clinics, and even helped in the O.R. when necessary. Throughout this experience, my desire to enter the medical profession only increased as I saw the incredible opportunity for service intrinsic in a medical career.

My second goal consisted of attending an excellent graduate school in the fields of history, my major topic of study, or in international relations, my area of career expertise. I was given the opportunity to attend Yale University's graduate program in International Relations this year and decided that it was a chance of which I had to take advantage. I spoke with several medical school representatives and indicated that I wished to merely work toward my masters for one to two years before returning to medical school. My experience at Yale has further expanded my knowledge of myself and the world and further prepared me for life as a medical professional. After having completed these two secondary goals in my life, I am entirely ready to pursue the primary, that of becoming a physician. Upon my entrance to medical school, I will now have no regrets, nor will I have any reservations.

Many reasons come to mind when I ask myself why I desire to become a physician, but only a few when I consider why it is that I should be allowed to enter medical school. I believe that a good physician need not be brilliant, but must be intelligent and exhibit discernment in difficult situations. However, every physician must possess endurance and the ability to care. There are difficult times in the life of every physician and every medical student, and not every situation is rewarding. During these trials, a strong sense of duty and perseverance are all that physicians can rely upon to fulfill their responsibilities. Finally, a physician must possess the ability to care. Again, in some situations it may seem difficult to provide attentive treatment, but a physician must be able to overcome the situation and fulfill the duties of a care-giver. As a prospective medical student, I believe I possess the perseverance and the ability to learn to care that are requisite for a career as a physician.

E s s a y   # 1 9

I have never understood the great hullabaloo some people raise about a conflict between science and the humanities. All my life I have been attracted to both and am puzzled by the perspective of a friend who claims, "I'm not a 'science person'," or some of my fraternity brothers who raise their brows when I register for a class in poetry writing. As a profession, I feel medicine will allow me to live in both worlds.

I enjoy learning about lots of different things, so school has always been easy and fun. I also take great pride in being competent in many areas, from basketball and windsurfing to tutoring math and cooking chicken paprikash. For as long as I can remember, I have been an addict of the animal shows appearing on television. I love watching polar bears plunging through ice and closeups of frogs laying jelly-covered eggs. But I never aspired to be shooting those films, knee deep in mire or perched in a tree, and I don't want to be a veterinarian. When I first entered high school I wanted to direct films, modeling myself after Francois Truffaut. Later I decided I would satisfy this desire with artful home movies or perhaps by assisting in a medical documentary. Writing fiction is one of my favorite hobbies and I would love, some day, to try publishing a novel.

Of all my interests, I have a special passion for biology which I expect everyone to share. The magic in living things which transcends molecular and cellular analysis makes studying them the most interesting thing I can imagine. So when someone blurts, "Ugh! I hated biology in high school!" I smile but honestly wonder if he is crazy. My research experience of two summers in a neuroimmunology lab at Columbia intensified this conviction and made me even more excited about my plans to study medicine.

There is a tradition of doctors on both the Cuban and Hungarian sides of my family, but it was only late in high school that I decided for sure that I wanted to study medicine myself. When my older brother, now studying at Mount Sinai, decided to go into medicine, I chose all my high school courses in areas outside natural science. Gradually, I realized that I could still like science, or consider a medical career, without just copying my brother. Volunteering in the emergency room at Columbia Presbyterian last summer was the final step I needed to evaluate my commitment to medicine and it has made me sure that I am doing the right thing. I sought out the smelliest and bloodiest patients, changing their bed pans and bringing them water, and once helped restrain a woman having heart seizures while blood streamed from a catheter in her nose. I found that actively helping made these experiences less and less gross and unexpectedly emboldened me to tackle something bigger. I was also inspired by the exciting side of medicine, rushing to the trauma room in any free moment to watch the surgeons clean and stitch wounds. Sometimes I caught myself grinning on the subway ride home, wondering if some day I would be sewing wounds myself.

Though I welcome excitement and intellectual satisfaction, what I really want from my career is to feel I am channeling a lifetime of energy into something meaningful and worthwhile. As compared to a career in business, or directing films, I believe studying and practicing medicine will fulfill this need. The greatest asset I have to offer is my motivation, to give and to work, to become as good a doctor as I am able to. Beside a warm family and close friends, there is truly nothing I want more and nothing that would make me happier.

E s s a y   # 2 0

*T*he rate at which medical knowledge is moving along today has brought out the necessity for two very important qualities in physicians: an open mind, which will recognize the advantages and, at the same time, limitations of new technologies and practicing methods, and a high degree of adaptability, which will allow these new methods to be effectively integrated into medical practice.

I believe that my life experience reflects such qualities. Throughout my education I have tried to keep an open mind and expand my horizons. Making the decision to come to the United States for my college education was a step in that direction. Prior to that, I had spent significant periods of time in Africa (Zambia, Ghana and Morocco), and in travelling through Europe. My stay in Morocco was particularly interesting: I witnessed the efforts of an ambitious ruler to inspire a fascinating but at times distorting process of modernization along western models.

I spent the latter part of my schooling at Campion School in Athens, Greece, which prepares students according to the British educational system. Although my high school community was small and rather close knit, its environment was limiting only to those who chose to find limits in themselves. Besides my placing first in my graduating class, I was active in student government, classical drama, three varsity sports, and classical guitar performances. At the same time I came to develop a keen interest in the biological sciences and a fascination for the humanitarian aspects of medicine.

Coming to the University of Pennsylvania to explore the field of Biology was a major decision which I took, conscious of the new directions it would open up for me. The environment was quite different from any other I had known before, but I needed the challenge to see how valuable my previous experiences really were. After all, my intention had always been to build for myself a perspective which would give me a good degree of awareness and adaptability. Admission to the highly competitive University Scholars program and my success in gaining a place on the varsity soccer team placed me in a very challenging milieu within the university. I believe I responded well. Academically, my program of liberal arts studies reached deep into the process of intellectual enrichment which I consider to be basic to the notion of scholarship. In sports, I became the top varsity goal-scorer and was voted most improved player.

My motivation is a tool which I love to put to use in causes that I feel are worthwhile. This is reflected in the significant broadening of activities at the Penn Greek Club when I took office as President. We began to organize a series of lectures and films on issues as diverse as recent political developments in Greece, the restoration of Athenian monuments, and the Olympic theme. The response was quite rewarding: our club membership eventually tripled.

I have come to regard medicine as a field where the practitioner is in a constant, intimate relationship with science while drawing on much more than just pure science. This dialectic process holds a special appeal for me. In my mind, emphasis in medical care should be as much on "care" as on the "medical" or scientific aspect. Furthermore, I recognize medicine as a field flexible enough for one to follow his own particular course, and even open up new ways. I see, for example, that in the future the dedicated physician may need to become more and more associated to the statesman and the lawmaker; the effects that medical advances have in shaping society and culture are too great for medicine to be regarded solely as an intellectual enterprise. This of course entails expanded responsibilities. I feel capable of contributing to the undertaking.

Essay #21

During the past year, as I was finalizing decisions about my career choice, I have had to accept a more realistic picture of the medical profession than one I had in the past. Based on talks I have had with some physicians, I have gained a better understanding of some of the current problems in medicine. I have also gained a better appreciation of the dedication and devotion of these physicians. These conversations, which at first shocked me, eventually fueled a growing interest that I had in medicine.

Though a medical career had been a consideration since high school, it remained one of several considerations until I began to concentrate in the sciences and accumulate some experience in the area during college.

During the summer of my sophomore year at Cornell, I worked in a reagents research and development lab for a supplier of hospital diagnostic equipment. After deriving improved reagents for spectrophotometric blood analyzers, I tested the accuracy of the new formulas. My summer at Instrumentation Labs proved helpful in future work because I had a chance to familiarize myself with a more sophisticated lab.

In the spring of my junior year I worked with Dr. W.R. Butler of the Physiology Department at Cornell, researching endogenous opiates in rats. In addition to localizing a source of the opiates in the adrenal medulla, I was able to achieve an acetylcholine dependant surge in opiate secretion from the adrenal. Dr. Butler guided me in establishing a credible experimental design, and technicians have introduced me to a number of relevant assay techniques. In the fall, I will be investigating the possible role of opiates integrated with pituitary and/or hypothalamic hormones in regulating the stress response of rats.

This past summer I worked in the Thyroid Diagnostic Center of the Brigham and Women's Hospital. I studied deiodination of thyroid hormone (mainly in the form of T4) to triiodothyronine (T3). T3 has been shown to be a much more active form of the hormone, but T4 is the more predominant thyroid product, thus the conversion is important physiologically. An enzyme similar to the one responsible for the deiodination leading to most of the circulating T3 has been found in brown adipose tissue and may be involved in non-shivering thermogenesis. I investigated the effects of various hormonal treatments on this enzymatically mediated conversion and described receptor mechanisms operating in isolated cells. I have learned conventional biochemical lab procedures, such as RIA's and electrophoresis techniques, and have also had the chance to absorb some of the expertise of the physicians and Ph.D's with whom I have worked. Additionally, while at Brigham and Women's, I have attended lectures given by hospital and lab personnel.

This recent experience has served to focus my career interests. While in school I have enjoyed studying endocrinology and immunology, and I would like to go on to study internal medicine. Eventually, I want to work in a university affiliated hospital, and to be involved in clinically related research, while maintaining patient contact.

At Cornell I have probed some of my other interests, including economics, psychology and politics, as well as taken rigorous science courses which have prepared me well for the demanding curriculum at medical school. I have been an ambassador for the Arts and Sciences School for the past two years during which I have housed prospective Cornellians and have given tours to their families. Also, as a Biology Student Advisor, I have been responsible for advising a group of ten freshmen each year about the biology program at Cornell. This school year I will be a Resident Advisor in a predominantly freshman dorm. I expect the challenges and rewards to be tremendous.

Medicine interests me because it is often adjusting to new technology and ideas. A career in medicine excites me, not only because of my interests but because it is an opportunity for me to do something I think I could do well while deriving the gratification that comes from helping people.

E s s a y   # 2 2

I find myself trying to answer the question "Why do you want to be a doctor?" Such a question seems to demand an organized and logical response which I can produce without much trouble, but which is only answers instead of reasons: "I am interested in sciences; I like people; I think it would be exciting." My own answer to myself is more simple, yet more inexplicable—simply that the closer I get to medical practice, the more I like it and the better "gut-feeling" I get about my decision to pursue it. It is our feelings we react to; the justification comes afterwards. Thus I find myself only able to offer a logical rationalization of the emotional responses that are my actual motivation to pursue medicine.

In contrast to many of my fellow premeds at Cornell, I entered college with no intention of ever pursuing medicine as a career. I had always been interested in wildlife and environmental studies. I travelled as far as Maine and Alaska in ecological study programs. I taught myself taxidermy and museum preservation skills. In fact it was Cornell's reputation in ornithology that led me to Ithaca. Yet as I became more deeply involved in animal behavior studies, I started to feel a nagging uncertainty as to whether wildlife research was indeed all that I wanted. Realizing that I might be continuing in this study more by inertia than conviction, I decided to take a semester leave of absence to assist a Cornell doctoral student in his research on mockingbird behavior in Texas, hoping to decide whether I really wanted to continue in this direction. After a month or two of this research, I found that the aesthetics of the environment still moved me, but everyday we were working on the same problem, and it quickly became apparent that the results could never justify the effort to me. I grew frustrated with the often myopic intensity of this form of research, and the way an individual's success or failure seemed to depend only on the substance of his thesis, to the apparent exclusion of the content of his character.

Having abandoned what I had always assumed would be my destined career, I used much of my free time in Texas for introspection and soul searching, trying to decide what I wanted and valued in my life. It was a fascination with science that drew me into biology originally, and though pure research appears too tightly focused to satisfy me, I still enjoy studying science immensely. But I also know that science means more to

125

me if it is linked to individual people. I have decided that medicine or teaching would be the best way for me to stay involved in science, since each incorporates the humanistic qualities that pure research has not seemed to require; and knowing myself, I think that I will be more happy as the doctor rather than the teacher.

My experience this summer has given me added confidence in my decision to pursue medicine. I have been working as a surgical scrub tech in the Johns Hopkins Hospital Gynecology Operating Room. Every day I am scrubbed and in the middle of surgery, sometimes for six hours at a time, handing instruments, threading sutures, retracting, and always asking questions. I have never enjoyed a job more and I truly can't think of anything I would rather be doing this summer (and certainly nothing else that would get me out of bed at 5:30 a.m. every day). Even when I know nothing about the patient, the science and the surgical technique are fascinating, but when I can talk to the patient and develop at least some personal contact, the science suddenly becomes medicine and it takes on new meaning, for it is that personal contact that moves me the most.

When Helen Avery said goodbye to me for this summer with tears in her eyes, saying she didn't know what she was going to do without me, I realized the feeling that is probably my strongest motivation. She is 87 years old, with two artificial knees, and the beginnings of Parkinson's disease, but she is still the sharpest of all the elderly that I visited last year. Every Friday afternoon I went to see her, sometimes to go for a walk, sometimes to take her shopping, but mostly just to talk. I cannot describe how good it felt to know that my presence mattered, to see her light up and smile when she opened the door for me. As a doctor, hopefully, I can find that feeling again and again. The science may interest me, the diagnoses may challenge me, but it will be that personal involvement with the patient that will make the most difference to me and keep me going through the hardest parts.

E s s a y # 2 3

M y interest in the field of medicine is the product of a lifelong process of discovery which began when I was a child. My mother, a clinical pathologist, and my father, a research pathologist, were responsible for many of the early experiences which sparked my interest in medicine. Through such experiences, I was exposed to many facets of the field, from wondrous triumphs to harsh realities. As a child, I would frequently visit my parents' laboratories. My father would demonstrate the uses of many modern pieces of equipment, often allowing me to look through his electron microscope, while my mother would show me her patients' slides, explaining the reasons for the various and too often malignant diagnoses.

My summer experiences have given me several opportunities to examine the field of medicine firsthand. During the past three summers, I have worked at NYU Medical Center on projects which have provided me with some perspective on both the clinical and basic science aspects of medicine. At the Rusk Institute, I worked with a team which rehabilitated stroke and accident victims, both physically and emotionally, and I thus became familiar with some of the basic requirements of patient care. In the Department of Hematology, my research for the past two summers focused on the glycoprotein IIb-IIIa complex, which comprises the fibrinogen receptor site on the surface of the platelet membrane. One aspect of this research dealt with investigating the mechanism of Post Transfusion Purpura, a platelet incompatibility disorder caused by PLA1, an antigen present on most individuals' glycoprotein IIIa. Consequently, I performed numerous experiments utilizing electrophoresis techniques as well as monoclonal antibodies in Western Blot procedures.

While these projects have served to confirm the intellectual basis for my interest in medicine, nonacademic events have shaped my emotional commitment to the field. Through my three-year participation in the Veterans Administration Hospital Volunteers Program, I have derived immense satisfaction by providing conversation and companionship to lonely elderly patients and younger veterans with psychiatric disorders. At the Rusk Institute, I was able to witness and share in the joy patients feel upon slowly regaining strength in their limbs. All of these experiences have made me dramatically aware that physicians have an unparalleled opportunity to help others; this prospect, more than any other, has become my major inducement towards a career as a physician.

E s s a y # # 2 4

I have been a springboard diver for half of my life. I started at age ten, and by the time I was thirteen I was training six days a week, not because my coach or my parents told me to, but because I loved it. Diving has been my most consistent undertaking over the years; it is the unifying thread that has not only given me immense pleasure, but that has also helped me to grow and to become the person I want to be. As I look back, I see the few material gains diving has given me, such as travel and college offers, but more importantly, I see the vast personal gains it has provided: The ability to do hard work, the ability to honor a commitment, the mastery of fear, the experiences of success and self-confidence, and the ability to achieve, to be successful in the face of competition, the ability to sacrifice to achieve the goals I have set.

Diving has given me much, but it has not always been fun. The competition and the mastery of a new dive are what make the sport worthwhile for me, but to achieve these moments of beauty, long hours of practice are necessary—through the winter months, through the times when my friends were out enjoying themselves, through the times when I was not well or was tired. To succeed, I have had to set hard, specific goals for myself, such as becoming a High School All-American (which I achieved), winning the New York State Empire Games (which I did), qualifying for the NCAA Division I Championships (which I have not yet done), and becoming an NCAA All-American (which I most probably will never be). When I think about sleeping and missing a morning workout, or going off with my friends, I recall my goals and realize that I need every bit of practice I can get. Diving has made me realize something that guides me throughout my life: If I want to achieve badly enough, I must make sacrifices now to reach my goals.

As I have progressed, I have gained self-confidence and pride from my ability to work hard for what I want. Also, I have over and over conquered an emotion that feels good to conquer, fear; fear of hitting the board, fear of hitting the water, fear of being out of control 33 feet in the air, fear of performing and exposing my inner self to crowds, fear of failure. I, and all other divers, have experienced all these, many times over. I have really hurt myself, really embarrassed myself. What has been most important to me, though, is the ability I have gained to force myself back up there, to try the dive again, to dive in front of the same old crowd the next week. When I can, and can later succeed, the fear goes away, and the confidence in overcoming the fear grows.

Diving has taught me, too, the concept of balance. In college we work out from three to five hours a day, and from December to March have long trips to compete elsewhere. I, like all athletes, have learned how to study when I am tired after workouts. I have learned how to dive and live my life at the same time, how to study and have fun while upholding the athletic standards I have chosen. I have also learned how to maintain my body and my mind, how to elicit the best performance possible, and how to remain healthy when my performance or the team's success depends on it. I have learned to think when I am tired.

I have been successful at the sport, and it has influenced my way of life and my ways of thinking. I believe the qualities that I have gained from diving will help me to be successful in medicine. I have the ability to work hard, experience physical discomfort and mental fatigue, and continue to think and perform well. I can make sacrifices to achieve goals I believe in. I believe that I have the maturity and emotional stability to cope with the rigors of a doctor's education and life, and the personal integrity that will enable me to uphold the trust and responsibility placed in a doctor. And I will always retain my sense of balance—to take all that life can throw at me and turn it to my best advantage. Diving and medicine are both paradoxical—one must strive for perfection, but must realize that perfection will never be reached. To succeed in medicine is my main goal for the rest of my life; it is a goal I believe I can achieve.

Essay #25

My growing up in a medical family was probably what provided the initial impetus for my interest in a medical career. However, it is my own experiences, apart from my family, which have made it clear to me that this choice is truly based on what I want to do with my life.

My mother is a physician and she has provided a meaningful role model for me. I was aware throughout of her ability to combine concern for helping people with their medical problems with a strong concern for each individual. I was impressed with her investment in seeing that each patient received the best possible medical care and her ability to combine patient care with ongoing research—research which led to some significant contributions in the area of treatment. My father's position, as I was growing up, as the Medicaid administrator for the city, brought home to me the issues related to equitable delivery of medical care. His devotion of much of his adult life to a program that was a step in the direction of providing medical care for all people in need, regardless of income or insurance regulations, has hopefully made a difference in people's lives.

It is the experiences which I have had, however, which have been important in furthering my understanding of the complexities and realities of the life of a physician. The volunteer work which I did at the Health Sciences Center exposed me to the kind of research which needs to be ongoing in relation to medical problems, and which ultimately contributes to improved patient care. The painstaking work which I was engaged in, in translating CAT scan data onto computers, was part of an attempt to clarify how bone conformation relates to locomotion. I can see such data being used in a variety of preventive ways—in rehabilitation after injuries, in determining the amount of stress an athlete can withstand and in cases of osteoporosis, among others.

My work in the Orthopedic Department at County Medical Center has shown me even more sharply than any previous experience, the complex nature of the skills which contribute to making the competent, caring physician. The in-depth understanding of the human body, the complicated skills needed in performing surgery and the need to find ways of dealing with the tragedies which physicians are confronted with, present a lifelong challenge. To see a 30-year-old woman die on the operating table after having jumped in front of a train makes one wonder what was going on in her life that led her to do this. But it is also clear that while the physicians were working to save her, the need was to focus on the medical-surgical tasks confronting them. I could see that the young men who become paraplegic and quadriplegic as a result of motorcycle and water accidents need doctors who can help them with their medical needs and help them go on with their lives. But maybe doctors can also play a role in education for prevention.

I believe at this time that my interest lies in orthopedics. However, I am aware that much lies before me as I hope to start my medical education, and that I need the education, training and exposure to the full range of medicine, before making a lifelong commitment to a specialty.

E s s a y # 2 6

*M*y interest in medicine has developed over many years. As a child and adolescent, my parents and relatives filled our home with keen and insightful discussion of the profession. Both of my grandfathers were doctors, two of my uncles are cardiologists, and on one side of the family the tradition goes back four generations—when medicine could hardly claim to be a science.

The decision, however, to become a physician has developed in college as an ungentle fusion of my two majors: physics and English. I refrained from a conservative curriculum at the undergraduate level and this combination allowed me a full dose of the humanities and a strong foundation in the physical sciences.

While I continue to enjoy the abstract nature of these disciplines, I consider medicine the practical union of these academic interests: scientific procedures will produce undeniable results, and yet behind each physical ailment will be an individual with special needs and priorities. The double-edged nature of the health profession requires a divided perspective.

My summer work over the last several years further guided my interests in medicine. As a YMCA camp counselor, I gained great satisfaction working closely with others. Moreover, the importance of qualified medical attention and knowledge was driven home to me. As waterfront director, I taught Advanced Lifesaving to all the staff. One summer, one counselor dove into shallow water and injured his neck. A recently trained counselor recognized the cause of his friend's inactive prone position and carefully turned him over allowing him to breathe until the paramedics and doctor arrived to safely immobilize his neck.

Two summers ago, while working on a survey crew on a remote Navajo reservation in Arizona, I was fascinated by the need for culturally sensitive medical care. Good doctors there learned to explain their work and ask questions in ways that demonstrated an understanding of and a respect for a proud culture. Yet the need for primary care physicians was painfully obvious; the bubonic plague made its appearance several times that summer.

This past summer, I was privileged to work in West Germany with two renal physiologists, Dr. Beyenbach of Cornell University and Dr. Fromter of the Max Planck Institute. Earlier that year I had gained general

133

lab experience working in Dr. Beyenback's lab at Cornell. Because of this experience, they allowed me to work quite independently to develop my own skills of physiological investigation.

Our main interest was ion specific channals present in the membranes of collecting duct cells in the mammalian kidney. To study channals, we employed the rather recent technique of patch clamp as developed by the German physiologist Neher. This technique uses tiny glass pipettes to electrically isolate small portions of a cell membrane. Channals can then be detected by the small currents that arise when ions of a specific polarity flow through the small pores of the membrane. I will present the results of this research this December at the American Society of Nephrology's Annual Meeting.

While my work this past summer proved my general abilities in research, I plan to practice medicine at the clinical level. Several factors influence this choice. First of all, I am a person of practical abilities. Although I often enjoy theoretical considerations, I consider myself to be most effective and useful dealing with individual problems. Secondly, I enjoy involvement with a variety of people and a variety of problems. Finally, I favor a more holistic approach in medicine, and toward that end I intend to practice primary-care medicine as a Family Practitioner.

Essay #27

A successful and effective physician must possess two essential qualities—a thirst for knowledge, and a deep motivation to aid his fellow man. Unfortunately, today's stereotypical "premed" student seems altogether preoccupied with the former at the exclusion of the latter. While a good doctor must possess an innate intelligence and an ability to expand and update his knowledge, it is equally important that he or she be able to effectively interact and communicate with the coworkers and patients that surround him. I believe my experiences and accomplishments at Cornell show that I possess both the necessary desire and essential skills needed to succeed in the field of medicine.

In satisfying my thirst for knowledge, I have pursued a broad range of courses end employment that demonstrate my raw abilities. Science has always fascinated me, and I think my academic choices reflect those interests. In addition, I have acted as a research assistant for the past two summers under Dr. Stefen Cohen of the University of Buffalo Department of Medicine at Buffalo General Hospital, examining the tumoricidal effects of isolated liver cells. My work culminated with the acceptance of a paper, which I coauthored, entitled "Augmentation of Natural Cytotoxicity of Murine Nonparenchymel Liver Cells by Interferon or Interleukin 2" for publication this fall in Sinusoidal Liver Cells by Elsevier Biomedical Press.

To be an informed participant in contemporary society, though, requires more than just scientific intelligence and rote memorization. To fully appreciate that being we call man, one must have experience in the informed reflection upon the literature, philosophy, and art of our society, as well as an understanding of politics, history, end economics. The broad range of academic and extracurricular activities I have pursued in college demonstrates my desire to gain an extremely comprehensive exposure to such material, as well as the skills to solve problems and process information.

But knowledge in and of itself is insufficient. I perceive knowledge not as an end, but as a means to an end—helping people. A simple glance at the activities I have participated in at Cornell clearly illustrates how crucial others are to me, and I think there is one obvious conclusion—I like people! Whether it's teaching, helping, entertaining, talking, or just enjoying a good laugh, I am comfortable, confident, end effective interacting with other people. I am a member of the Delta Chi fraternity, where I have acted as Alumni Secretary, Corresponding Secretary, and a member of the Executive Board. I have been quite active as a College Ambassador, hosting potential students and giving tours to visitors at Cornell. I have also acted as a student advisor, advising students on various aspects of Cornell—whether it be scheduling problems or just roommate trouble. On campus I've held a number of jobs, and have also acted as a teaching assistant for an Oral Communications class. In addition, I am presently acting as a TA for both an Animal Physiology Laboratory and a Microcomputer Applications course. Each of these activities requires not only a considerable amount of responsibility, but a good deal of patience as well.

By far the most enjoyable (and time-consuming) activities I am involved in have been singing with the Cornell Glee Club, and a small men's *a cappella* subset called the HANGOVERS—known both for our singing and our sense of humor. In more than three years of activity, we have toured California, the Southeastern U.S. and various portions of the Northeast, released an album, and performed for nume-rous gatherings of students, alumni, and friends, as well as the likes of Helmut Schmidt, Henry Kissinger, Gerald Ford, and Bob Hope.

Clearly, I have not allowed myself to become trapped in the static environment of the "preprofessional" student. I have managed to both expand my scope of knowledge and grow as an individual. Yet throughout this whole process I have also managed to focus my interests and intensify my desires. Without hesitation, I can honestly say that there can be no better choice for me than a career in medicine, for medicine combines the best of both worlds—working closely with people while continuing in a scientific field. I firmly believe I have the ability to succeed in such a career, and will find great satisfaction in patient care. Through a career in medicine I can help man at his most basic level, his physical presence, and still grow individually while contributing to society's wealth of knowledge.

While intent on pursuing an active practice, possibly in pediatrics, orthopedics, oncology, or geriatrics, I fully intend to incorporate both clinical and experimental research into my work. Farther down the road, I would like to become involved in public policy as it relates to health care and science. It seems fairly obvious that governmental legislation and policy has lagged far behind the advances being made in many scientific fields, and needs to be updated. While active medical practice is my primary goal, I feel that I could contribute significantly to both the scientific community and the general public by acting as an advocate for science among the politicians.

E s s a y   # 2 8

A t age fifteen I found myself flat on my back in an emergency room, uncertain if I would ever walk again. I had just learned that I suffered a compression fracture in my lower back. It was a very frightening experience that would change the course of my life. The physicians at Vanderbilt University Hospital worked hard to allay my fears and ensure a full recovery. I saw personal qualities in the doctors that I wanted to emulate in my own life. I knew then I wanted to pursue a career in medicine.

As a child, I participated in projects directed at helping the less fortunate in my community. I gained an awareness and respect for others by giving of myself to help improve the quality of life of those around me. At an early age, I was motivated to take an active role in improving the human condition. The misfortune of my accident at fifteen afforded me a glimpse into the profession that would enable me to realize this goal.

I began college several years after graduating from high school. I had been on my own since before high school graduation and was working to support myself and save money for college. I have supported myself throughout college, usually working two or more jobs to pay tuition and my living expenses. Balancing work and school proved challenging, requiring me to continually mature as a person and a student. The obstacles I have encountered have underscored my determination and commitment to becoming a physician. I have remained focused and determined to reach my goal. I believe perseverance, maturity, dedication, drive and commitment are among the attributes I will bring to the medical profession.

My interest in medicine has continued to develop through my volunteer work and my basic microbiological research. As a volunteer in the Cuddler program for the Neonatal Unit at Methodist Hospital Dallas, I have been inspired by the impact that physicians have on the lives of their patients. I have seen first hand the importance of a compassionate approach to patient care and the nurturing role of a physician. I am drawn to medicine's demand for excellence and pursuit of perfection. At the same time, my research experiences have improved my capacity to assimilate information and apply it to more practical situations. During my summer internship under the direction of Justin Radolf, M.D., at The University of Texas Southwestern Medical Center at Dallas, I investigated a family of outer membrane-associated lipoproteins involved in immune evasion by Treponema pallidum and Borrelia burgdorferi, causative agents of venereal syphilis and Lyme disease, respectively. At the University of Texas at Arlington, I investigated the highly selective and regulated membrane transport mechanisms involved in maintaining Magnesium homeostasis and its role as a possible virulence factor. I believe that the practice of medicine and scientific research go hand in hand. During my medical training, I look forward to being able to combine my love of science with my enthusiasm for medicine as a healing art.

Medicine is a rewarding and humbling career that will enable me to touch peoples lives in a way not possible with other professions. I have the compassion, emotional stability and stamina to excel in the study and practice of medicine. My desire to contribute to the wellness of my community and passion for medicine makes becoming a physician the right choice for me.

E s s a y   # 2 9

I t has been my ambition, for some time, to become involved in the medical profession. I chose medicine because I feel it is my duty in life to concern myself with the well being of others. This duty can best be fulfilled to my satisfaction by pursuing a career in medicine.

To fulfill my aspirations there are certain key qualities that I must acquire. I have begun to prepare for that responsibility by maintaining a strong academic background and involving myself in extracurricular activities and clinical experiences.

My undergraduate education has provided a strong background for my future studies in medical school. With a B.S. in Microbiology, I have acquired an in-depth knowledge of the biological sciences. I have been able to improve my research and scientific skills by applying the knowledge to my Microbiology lab work with pathogenic organisms, such as *Neisseria gonorrhoea.*

The life of a good, dedicated physician involves more than knowing how the body functions. Equally important is knowing how to deal with people on a personal basis. I have acquired some clinical experience in the area of interpersonal relationships. Two years ago I volunteered as a nurses' aid at a local hospital. I worked primarily with elderly patients and became more sensitive to their special needs. This summer I am working as a volunteer in an Emergency Room. This experience has given me the opportunity to observe doctors and nurses in critical situations. I am also working with a doctor in his private practice. My duties involve filing charts, assisting patients, urine and stool analysis and developing X rays. I feel these experiences are invaluable to me in developing a sensitivity to patients and their needs.

My ethnic background has been a contributing factor in my prospective plan after medical school. I would like to work in a physician shortage area where a Puerto Rican background will be helpful in dealing with other Hispanic minorities.

I want to succeed in my career goals. I will be a successful doctor if I am able to give the sick the compassion and quality medical care that they deserve.

Essay #30

Simply stated, childhood accidents and subsequent visits to pediatricians, dentists, and hospitals established my interest in medicine. During these sessions, I was slowly exposed to many disciplines of practical medicine—radiology, anesthesiology, thoracic surgery, plastic surgery, emergency room medicine, and orthopedics. Although the visits themselves were not unusual for an active child, my enthusiasm may have been so; a broken bone presented another chance to see "how doctors worked."

As I grew, so did my enthusiasm for medicine. Fortunately, this fervor also matured. To my delight, I found that I didn't have to break an arm or step on a rusty nail to learn a little bit more about medicine. I turned rather to books, magazines, journals, and other sources of information. Very quickly, it was clear that medicine was not just doctors and hospitals but that it pervaded society in a very broad sense. With that realization, I began a scholastic, physical, and emotional approach to an eventual career in medicine.

During the second half of my freshman year at the University of Michigan, I applied for and was awarded a competitive premedical/medical scholarship through the United States Air Force. A part of this application required me to write a tentative plan of study for the following undergraduate years. This outline has served as the basis for my directed liberal-arts education. My studies have included subjects from molecular biology to astronomy and from comparative politics to the literature of Thomas Mann. This Summer, I have supplemented these studies with practical laboratory experience both full-time in immunology under Dr. Latham Claflin and on a volunteer basis in Dr. Benedict Lucchesi's pharmacology laboratory.

Because I am most mentally fit when I am physically fit, my undergraduate years have also included a host of recreational and competitive sports. Regular tennis and squash matches as well as seasonal competition on the University of Michigan Rowing Team, therefore, have also contributed to my approach toward medicine.

Emotionally, there are both planned and unplanned events which prepare me for that side of medicine. Among those planned are challenging academic schedules as well as a year of study in Freiburg, West

Germany. Occasionally, each of these examples was a source of stress and anxiety to be overcome. Planned psychological challenges, however, are often dwarfed by those not forecast. For many years, my father struggled to live with bipolar affective disorder and schizophrenia. As a family, we struggled with him. Last August, however, we had to involuntarily hospitalize him. He has since left our family. As the oldest of four children, I have been faced with both the loss of my father and a redefining of my role in the family. The events of this last year have caused me to question nearly everything I had taken for granted and have made me aware of unsuspected reservoirs of strength I had not known before.

I view my eventual career in medicine as one filled with both sacrifice and intangible reward. From broken bones and stepped-on rusty nails to directed collegiate years and unforseen tragedy, I have followed a pathway toward these sacrifices and gains. With all of the experiences which have prepared me for events to come, I anticipate four years of medical school with enthusiasm.

Essay #31

The greatest motivational factor in my pursuit of a medical career was my work experience with the DuPont Company in the Cornell Engineering Co-Op Program. The seven months of research I performed at DuPont impressed upon me the similarities between my Chemical Engineering background and the increasingly technical nature of medicine. I was a member of a research group actively involved in improving certain types of polymers for industrial, as well as medical, applications. Polymers of this type find use in medicine due to their inert properties in the human body and other biological environments. As a research engineer, I also had the opportunity to learn about innovations within DuPont's Biomedical Products research laboratories. Here, I became aware of improvements in biotechnology and computers that will inevitably have a significant impact upon the quality of health care. Through this work experience in the engineering field, however, I also recognized that I wanted a career which places a greater emphasis on human relationships. A career in medicine will allow me to work with and help people in a more direct manner than I found possible in my engineering work.

As a student at Cornell University, I received a broad exposure to a variety of scientific disciplines which are the basis of many of today's rapidly advancing medical technologies. My interests in organic chemistry, biochemistry, and the engineering sciences were particularly important in forming my decision to enter a health-related career. I consider medicine to be a means for me to apply these or similar sciences in a most fulfilling and humane manner. In addition, I believe that the practical nature of my engineering education has afforded me a superior problem solving ability that can be applied to medicine as well as other scientific fields.

After my formal education at Cornell, it was my intention to work two years in the engineering profession before entering medical school. During this time, I hoped to gain practical skills and management experience relevant to my future medical career. I worked for the Nestle Company following graduation as a manager-in-training in their food processing operations. At Nestle, I learned about the nutritional aspects of health and worked with people in my role as a supervisor.

After nine months with Nestle, I decided to accept another

143

management position in mechanical design and manufacturing with the Ulster Tool and Die Corporation in Kingston, N.Y. My technical work at this firm, designing and developing specialized machinery, has given me the valuable knowledge of how people interact with mechanical devices. More importantly though, this opportunity to manage people in a professional environment has proven to be a most challenging and enjoyable task, confirming my decision to pursue a health career. The consistently high level of performance expected of me as a manager and engineer in this business has been an excellent preparation for my future responsibilities as a physician.

While being employed by Ulster Tool and Die, I have been performing volunteer work in the Radiology Department of the Benedictine Hospital in Kingston, N.Y. My work here, transporting and assisting patients for testing, has increased my familiarity with hospital procedures and proven to be a personally rewarding experience for me. From these practical pursuits in the hospital, working directly with patients and observing first-hand the realities of hospital life, I have had a candid introduction to health careers.

These varied experiences have given me the opportunity to more clearly define my professional goals. The time I have spent since my graduation from Cornell has been particularly important to me for personal growth and for making a more informed decision towards medicine. My strong background in the basic sciences, and the practical work experience I have in both the chemical industry and the hospital, have motivated me to pursue a health career.

E s s a y # 3 2

··

I was born Dutch and spent the first nine years of my life in the Netherlands. At that time my father retired and took the family to France. We lived for fourteen years on the Swiss-French border outside of Geneva. The international atmosphere of Geneva was represented by the children at the International School of Geneva, where I was a student through high school. For example, one unique experience during high school was participating in the "Student United Nations." For three days students from several European schools acted as diplomats from the countries represented at the United Nations. The exposure and sharing of the varied culture, religions, traditions and languages has continued to help me to accept people for what they are and to be able to adjust more readily to diverse situations. By maintaining a certain level of academic achievement I was permitted to participate in sports. I enjoyed being a member of many teams especially, ski, basketball and track teams. I felt honored to be named sports woman of the year during my senior year. Although all sports brought me pleasure, skiing was my favorite. Therefore, I pursued it more intensely and eventually raced for the Dutch National ski team. At this level, skiing was demanding not only physically but also mentally. My memories of the pressure, losing as well as winning, but especially the comradery will always remain with me.

After high school I decided to continue my education at the University of Geneva. I had three particular interests: people, nature and sciences. Medicine was a serious consideration but due to the conservative attitude of my parents and Switzerland, the idea of a woman in medicine was not well supported. Without the obvious role models to look up to, I chose to study Biology. The University was rather academically oriented without emphasis on athletic or social activities. Nonetheless, I felt compelled to continue to compete in basketball, sailing and skiing. My last year of the University was spent involved in an independent research project in microbiology, the results of which were the basis of my thesis entitled "Analysis of the genetic polymorphism of the HLA-DRB genes coding for class II antigenes of the human histocompatibility complex." The research was fascinating and challenging but on the other hand I realized it was not as idealistic as I had imagined it to be. I liked the technology and knowledge involved in basic science but I found

145

myself missing a more direct interaction with people.

That same year in the laboratory, I met the most wonderful man in the world who is now my husband. Mark was a Fulbright Scholar from the United States doing a year of research in Geneva. Fortunately, I completed my studies at the same time Mark finished his research. Therefore, I was able to go with Mark to the United States in August 1983 when he started at Cornell Medical School. It was my first time in the United States and the transition was made easier by Mark, his family and the fact that two of my best friends from high school happened to live in New York at the time. Since I was not yet a permanent resident it was initially difficult to find a job. After several waitressing jobs, a cardiologist hired me as his secretary. It was all new to me but I enjoyed the work, especially the patient contact. The atmosphere revived my old interest in medicine and I decided to continue my education. Again I considered medical school, but the surgical assistant program seemed like a perfect compromise. Being newly married a particular concern of mine was having the time for a family in the future. A shorter education with some responsibility and patient contact made the role of a surgical assistant look ideal. I loved learning about the applications of science in medicine, mastering some surgical techniques, and especially my interaction with the patients on the wards. Unfortunately, I soon realized that our short didactic course led us to become more technically oriented rather than problem-solving members of the surgical team. I finally decided that I would never feel comfortable in this situation and that being an assistant would never satisfy me. Therefore, I quit the program to reevaluate my future plans.

This was not terribly difficult. By now I had had more exposure to the demands of medicine, what medicine represents, and had spent some time discussing the issues of women in medicine. Therefore, I now feel comfortable and excited about becoming a physician. So, with the support of Mark, I decided to pursue what deep inside I always wanted to do, apply for medical school.

E s s a y   # 3 3

I love to live. I love to feel the sweat drip down my face as I run the Campus Drive loop. I love the force of my heart beating as I check the outcome of my latest experiment. I love to feel the chills that go down my spine when a friend runs to me with shocking news. I have known those who cannot enjoy all the sensations of living, and I want to give the life I enjoy to those who cannot.

I didn't want to be a doctor. I wanted to be an artist. As a child, the faces of people enamored me—how they looked, how they watched, and how often they smiled. My father had been an artist, and I wanted to capture the essence of people the way he did. Although too often, I would get caught up in looking, knowing that I couldn't reflect the spirit of a person through a drawing. What captured me was the movement, not the stillness of life. Theories would spin in my head as to why people "ticked" in so many different rhythms.

As I began to study more the inner-workings of life—the immense universe of our body with its own living populations, the blueprints contained in every cell, and the fact that one small change in a molecule, a nucleic acid, could give or restrict life—I became enchanted. Human life impassioned me.

My experiences in medicine since have been both phenomenal and heart wrenching. I have seen children saved and babies expire—and still each day, each event, pushes me further into medicine. My first science position, as all have been since then, was in human genetics. As I learned techniques of restriction mapping at my bench, the mother who worked at the bench across from me taught me another perspective. Her daughter is missing part of her 18th chromosome and, subsequently, developed a number of physical and mental disabilities. This mother quit her developing career and jumped into graduate school to find out what the doctors couldn't tell her. Each week, she would take me to tour the Intensive Care Unit for newborns while the medical geneticist examined babies for deformities. To see their minuscule bodies and touch their loose skin always incited me to work harder in the lab.

The next year in that pediatric department, Dr. Celia Kaye changed my life. This metabolic geneticist, whom I had admired from afar, allowed me to work with and learn from her. Her PKU clinic had grown to be the largest and best in South Texas. This woman gives PKU children intelligence and parents peace. Every week, new families learned from her how to transform their lives for their health. She was the most outstanding teacher I have witnessed: Each word she spoke bore tenderness, and each touch gave comfort. I saw Dr. Kaye give life to her patients.

At Stanford now, I am captivated by the effort of which I've become a part. Every day, I test for DNA mutations of patients with whom I may have shaken hands within clinic the week before. Many don't know what causes their afflictions. They are asking us to figure it out. They may have dislocated lenses and heart problems, but a defect in the Fibrillin 1 gene cannot be found. Will it be more serious? Is a heart operation inevitable? Can the tall, spider-fingered boy feel the rim of the basketball hoop at the climax of the game, or must he sit on the sidelines for fear his aorta will burst?

I'm determined to help these kids find energy and confidence in their futures—as a doctor with a mind and a heart. Life is my passion. The constant overstimulation of thoughts, lives, and dreams that emit from the people in my life are what drives me to explore. Each person I meet changes my life in some way. In return, I give them what I have plenty of: strength and love. I want to be the mother, the teacher, the researcher— the Doctor.

E s s a y # 3 4

C ollege was not part of my future when I graduated high school in 1991. Although I continued my education in a high level program at Rabbinical College, the Lubavitch community to which I belong encourages social work rather than "secular" college. Young people travel across the world, developing social programs, organizing camps, and opening schools to spread Jewish learning.

I grew up in Vancouver, British Columbia, and San Diego, California, in a home that was open to all who wanted to experience Jewish life. My father, a rabbi and a charismatic teacher, has always had guests in our home, and my mother, a calculus teacher, works after school and during weekends helping her students. My family's lifelong social commitment, the values of my society—and being the oldest of seven children—have permanently inculcated in me a feeling of responsibility and compassion for others. My life would necessarily be one of social involvement.

When I was in Russia helping to establish an overnight camp in the mountains of Kazakstan for indigent children, I had an experience that changed my destiny. The first night of camp, a counselor ran over to me, telling me that a camper of his was having difficulty breathing. The child was having his first acute asthma attack and appeared cyanotic. The phone lines were down, and our camp vehicle was in the repair shop. As a life-guard, I was the only staff member who knew first aid, but I felt completely inadequate. I kept reviewing the protocols for artificial respiration that I thought I would need to perform once the child stopped breathing entirely. Through the night I desperately tried to help the camper, but to no avail. I will never forget the feeling of total helplessness. Thankfully, the asthma subsided at dawn and the camper went to the hospital for treatment. That night I made a promise to myself that I would learn medicine. I returned to America and started my college education.

My new passion to become a doctor led me to become an EMT, and I joined the Teaneck Volunteer Ambulance Corps. I have since been an active member. My greatest joy is being able to help people, stabilize emergency situations, and utilize all my capacities to insure proper care. The overnight shift enabled me to attend my classes and work during the day, but the shift is a very demanding one. I am constantly exposed to difficult middle-of-the-night calls, emergency situations, reduced manpower and other challenges. Above all, I've learned to think when I'm tired.

For the past year and a half, I worked in Cornell University as the department of Geriatrics administrator. The doctors in the Cornell labs with whom I worked, particularly Dr. Marc Weksler, were studying the immune system. Their love of research and dedication to their field was awe-inspiring. I was in a position to appreciate that their work was accomplished despite bureaucratic tangles, grants that came and went capriciously, long hours, and adverse conditions. In Cornell, I was introduced to the area of research concerning the effect of age on the immune system. A friend and I found in our lab work that monoclonal-B lymphocyte populations appear in the blood of humans as they age. This study will hopefully bring us closer to understanding illnesses that are found in an aging population.

My varied experiences have clearly directed me towards a life as a physician. I have undertaken rigorous courses in science, and enjoyed them immensely. I have continued my intensive studies in Rabbinical College, finding them intellectually stimulating. I have volunteered my time in hospitals, prisons, camps, and synagogues. I have taken difficult examinations after spending the night on emergency calls, and rushed from there to my duties at Cornell.

But the experience which seemed to me to be the most similar to that of the great responsibility that a physician must have was the summer I was the head lifeguard at a lakefront camp in Montreal, Canada, responsible for the safety of 400 individuals. I made decisions based on instinct and judgment throughout the summer, and felt the constant burden of insuring the safety of the children. I was nineteen years old then, but I grew up quickly.

I'm proud of what I've accomplished in the few years that I've been part of the greater scientific world. I can't wait to continue.

Essay #35

I grew up in the home of two physicians and witnessed the practice of medicine at a very young age. Late night telephone calls and beepers sounding during dinner caused me to acknowledge that my parents had accepted a stressful and demanding occupation. I not only admired their dedication to work, but the fact that they had immigrated to the United States with nothing but a degree in medicine. Their training as medical doctors allowed them to transcend international boundaries of race and culture to succeed in America. I saw that physicians are an essential part of every society because they heal and nurture the sick. By seeing my parents' accomplishments, I developed a sense of respect for the profession. As a result, I envisioned myself as a doctor at a young age.

Before I entered college, however, I did not have much exposure to careers other than medicine. I had decided that medicine was the one profession which encompassed science and humanities. I had a rigid plan for how I would prepare for a career in medicine while in college. I would study biology, do well in school, and pursue activities that could prepare me for my future. Fortunately, a wonderful revelation occurred; I realized that college would be my chance to explore new disciplines that might hold the same benefits as medicine. Thus, my career at MIT proved to be one of the most fascinating and miraculous journeys I have ever encountered. I was exposed to innovative technology and stimulating people. I learned not to assume anything but to constantly question everything. As a result, my ability to reason blossomed in college. These changes challenged my previous plans to become a physician and enabled me to delve into foreign subjects.

In particular, I chose to study Chemical Engineering rather than Biology. Engineering introduced a different approach to the application of scientific knowledge and relied on strong mathematical ability. As a chemical engineer, I explored many innovative fields while improving my analytical thought. I studied subjects, such as fluid mechanics and heterogeneous catalysis, that challenged my abilities to solve problems. Without argument, though, my most fascinating courses were in Biotechnology.

My interest in Biotechnology culminated in an undergraduate research experience in which I explored a field of chemical engineering that had direct applications to the treatment of disease. In my project, I developed a delivery system to be used when transporting DNA in gene therapy. I prepared small polymeric spheres that would protect genes when they were injected into cells. These particles encapsulated the genes but were small enough to bypass the body's foreign material defense mechanism.

At times, the research was very exciting. I was at the forefront of technology and was exploring uncharted territories in the field of drug delivery systems. The research I performed could have profound effects on all of humankind. However, when I worked alone at a lab bench, I felt completely separate from society. The motivation of helping other people was not always evident. I was dissatisfied and began to look to other things for personal fulfillment. These other aspects of my life made me realize that Chemical Engineering research alone would not be completely gratifying.

Music became an essential part of my life. I began to sing with the MIT Concert Choir and various small groups around campus. This interest continued to grow until I decided to pursue a dual degree in Music and Chemical Engineering. In retrospect, this was one of the best decisions I made in college. My quantitative engineering classes were supplemented with reflective, abstract courses in classical music. More importantly, the time I spent alone in the laboratory was balanced by personal interactions during rehearsals and concerts. Singing allowed me to study compositions and express my interpretations to other people. During a performance, I felt successful when the audience could understand the emotion I was trying to portray.

I learned that true fulfillment, for me, can only be achieved by sharing my talent and training with other people. This satisfaction can be felt most through direct personal contact. A career in medicine relies on these means for fulfillment. A physician offers knowledge and dedication and, in return, receives the gratification of making others feel better.

I am sure of my decision to pursue a career in medicine and am cultivating my understanding of the field. Through my exposure to medicine as a child, I saw the constant work that was required. From my summer position in a doctor's office, I tested my abilities to reassure and listen compassionately. And during my internship in Washington, DC, I hope to understand the American system of healthcare. As a doctor, it is imperative to understand the issues in health policy that will have an impact on the structure of healthcare in America.

I do not feel as if I am blindly heading down a path to my destiny but rather am educated in the many possible routes I can take. I will never regret studying new fields and as a result, look forward with excitement to the day I start my journey to becoming a physician. To me, being a doctor will bring together all the personal values that I strive for in everyday life—the pursuit of excellence, humility, and care. My parents understood the need for balance between these characteristics when they chose to study medicine and come to America. I, too, have developed a strong devotion to the development of dedication, knowledge, and compassion and hope that these characteristics will mature throughout my life.

Essay # 36

I have always been interested in science and have practiced studio art and have wrestled for ten years. But it is difficult to explain my interest in three such widely differing pursuits as part of an underlying state of mind. After some thought, I was surprised to realize that there is indeed a similar motivation for all three activities.

This motivation relates to a deep interest I have always had in mythology and science fiction. The stories that most appeal to me are of individuals alienated from, or cast into, an alien society, struggling to assert their independence and individuality. By suspending my disbelief, I can partake in the struggle of the fictional characters and feel their victories and defeats. Art, wrestling and science are all, in a sense, isolating activities, and each requires a great deal of discipline and training. One cannot paint a picture the first time one steps into a studio; nor can one wrestle well the first time on a mat. Research requires the patience to gather the proper data, and also creativity to interpret the data correctly. These three interests have served as my way of becoming in reality the adventurers I have read about.

Let me elaborate. Several months ago, I was busy writing my thesis. I have already spent the better part of a year gathering data and running assays in a laboratory, and all that was left was the interpretation of the data. I found that instead of dreading the long hours of writing and rewriting, I looked forward to it. I felt that I was fitting-in the final pieces of a large jigsaw puzzle or coming to the end of an intricate detective story, and it was exciting to watch the overall picture slowly emerge. The feeling, surprisingly, was akin to a feeling I often get whenever I draw an excellent picture or wrestle a perfect match. In all these instances, I achieve a certain rhythm and feeling of inspiration that enables me to work with a minimum of energy. It is said that long distance runners experience a feeling called "runners' high," that makes them addicted to their running. The high I experience when I wrestle and win a match, draw an excellent picture or piece together bits of research is just as addictive. When I read science fiction, I identify with the protagonist because I feel that the control and effort vital to their successes are similar to qualities in myself that enable me to spend ten hours straight working on a picture, or spend weeks preparing for a wrestling match.

I have always wanted to be a doctor because I have sensed that much of a doctor's work will satisfy me in the way that my other interests satisfy me. I am careful, however, not to confuse my love of adventure and fantasy with my reasons for wanting to be a physician. For a long time I had conceived of myself as going through the medical training process so that I could become a "doctor/hero." Wielding a shining scalpel, I would cure all of my patients' problems with stunning success. What I now realize is that for most of my future patients, there will be no one sure method of treatment, and many of them may not respond to treatment at all.

Thus, it is my feeling that a doctor should be more than a dispenser of health care; he should also take an active role in the health community. It seems to me that the rising cost of health care and increasingly bewildering technology have created a breach in the rapport between doctors and the public. Many patients feel that they have little control or understanding of their treatment. As a doctor, I may not be able to cure or even help all of my patients, but, if I can help to bridge the gap between my and my patients' knowledge, then I will be as satisfied as I ever was reading myths and fiction. When I am a physician, I feel that the discipline and control I have learned from my other interests will serve me well, but more importantly I feel that the enthusiasm and joy that I derive from these interests will also be an integral part of my life as a doctor. Hopefully, my future patients will sense my enthusiasm and be encouraged by it.

E s s a y # 3 7

W illiam Carlos Williams was a Pulitzer Prize winning poet known for making the ordinary extraordinary, for celebrating the rugged lives of struggling farmers and the poor working class, for telling us that "so much depends upon a red wheelbarrow." Many are familiar with Williams's literary work, but few know that the main tool of his trade was not a typewriter but a stethoscope. Williams was a doctor. He spent his days as a general practitioner in Paterson, New Jersey, attending to the medical needs of working-class families who often could not afford to pay him for his services, and he wrote at night after evening office hours. Driven by compassion and a deep love of humanity, Williams battled economic hardship and the early rejection of his work to become a respected writer and a beloved physician who toiled, selflessly and tirelessly, for his fellow man. As such, Williams is a personal hero and an inspiration, and his reasons for entering medicine, along with the ideas and idealism that drove him, echo my own in many ways.

For Williams, literature and medicine were inextricably linked. Each was based, at its roots, on a fascination and a deep respect for humanity. Moreover, both callings appealed to Williams's strong sense of duty to society. Just as for Williams, my interest in literature and my medical aspirations are both rooted in a fascination with mankind and a desire to help others. In high school, I found that novelists such as Joseph Heller and Kurt Vonnegut used fiction to reveal the absurdity of war and the resilience of the human spirit, and I learned literature's potential to influence society. Writers were artists who could better the world with their words and, for a while, I wanted to become one.

My love of fiction led me to continue studying literature in college and, eventually, to write my own fiction and major in English. But working closely with several professors in Stanford's Creative Writing Program showed me that many writers, even good ones, have a very difficult time getting published. The risk of not having an impact on society was too great. I decided to concentrate on the other profession that I had been contemplating since high school: medicine.

My medical aspirations are based, in large part, on my love of science. My seventh-grade Life Sciences teacher, Mr. Byhower, sparked this interest by impressing on me the importance of protecting the environment and the many creatures whose very existence is threatened by human encroachment. In high school, I became very involved with the school's Ecology Club and the local chapter of the Sierra Club. My school's three-week senior trip, in which my classmates and I backpacked through over ninety miles of Arizona wilderness, remains one of the most challenging yet rewarding experiences of my life: it enabled me to enjoy nature first-hand, and it taught me the importance of perseverance, working in a team, and taking things one step at a time (literally). In college, I have tried to share my appreciation of nature with inner-city children by teaching a class on science and nature at an East Palo Alto elementary school.

The science courses I have taken in college have enabled my love of nature to blossom into a deep appreciation for science. As I studied biology, I marveled at the intricate beauty of the immune system and the nephron and the complexities of animal behavior. I recently returned from a field seminar in Galapagos, and, because I had been studying evolutionary theory and doing research on cleaning symbiosis all quarter, it was one of the most incredible experiences of my life.

Another important development in my education that helped convince me to pursue a medical degree has been my participation in community service. In high school, I tutored socio-economically disadvantaged students in mathematics and reading, and I felt, for the first time, the unique sense of happiness that arises from helping others. Practicing medicine struck me as a perfect combination of service and science, and my experiences in the medical field have shown this to be true. In the last few years, I have done volunteer work for a local pediatrician, Dr. Nguyen, and at the Packard Children's Hospital at Stanford. Working with young patients in the oncology clinic has been incredibly fulfilling, and it has taught me the importance of compassion in medicine. This summer, I have an even greater opportunity to witness doctor-patient interaction and the practice of medicine working with Dr. Ronald Wender at Cedars-Sinai Medical Center.

I know that I will encounter many difficulties as a medical student and, later, as a physician, especially with the way health care is changing in the U.S. today. But I think that it is still true that, as a doctor, I will be able to dedicate myself to helping others. Like Williams, I will still find time to write. I may not write the Great American Novel, but I will still be serving society, day in and day out, and that is what matters.

Essay #38

Although I have learned a great deal through formal course work, this has provided only a part of my education. During the past year, I have had the opportunity to work in an operating room and an emergency room of hospitals at home and at college. Although quite different, both were valuable learning experiences. In the operating room, I was able to observe how the hospital staff worked together in performing the mechanics of an operation. The emergency room, on the other hand, allowed me to see the impact that illness had on the patient and those close to him. These experiences have taught me that in addition to mastering the technical skills, success is dependent on the personal qualities of the physician. These qualities include compassion, emotional strength, and the ability to instill confidence in people.

I have developed some of these personal qualities in my work as a camp counselor for underprivileged children and as a Big Brother to a young boy living near my college. These experiences have also allowed me to know the feeling of having people depend on me, which is an important aspect of being a physician.

This summer I am working in a laboratory at The Sloan-Kettering Cancer Institute. I have always had a strong interest in research. I believe that investigative work helps build an inquiring, independent, and analytical approach to learning while developing the ability to evaluate and solve problems with ingenuity. The rapid therapeutic advances of today make this an asset, not only in academic careers such as medical research and teaching, but in clinical practice as well.

My parents are physicians so I have always been exposed to the field of medicine, a field which has interested me for much of my life. The past few years have provided opportunities for me to test this interest and strengthen my decision to pursue a career in medicine. It is a career which I am confident will provide numerous challenges and a lifetime of learning.

Essay #39

As a person who is highly interested in the sciences and in people, a career in medicine has always appealed to me. The ability to heal the sick is a gift I hope to attain and put to use. As time passes, I am more eager to become a surgeon and to practice medicine in or near a large city.

My first medical related experience occurred in the summer after my sophomore year of high school. I participated in the American Foundation for Negro Affairs Program (AFNA). This program supported the idea that more minorities were needed in the medical profession and financed tours of medical schools, showed filmstrips of surgical procedures, and presented lectures by medical doctors. AFNA increased my interest in medicine tremendously and was a major influence in my decision to become a doctor.

During my junior year, I became a volunteer worker at Lafon Nursing Home in New Orleans where I worked closely with the nurses and residents. This not only required me to learn several duties of nursing, but also taught me to become patient, understanding, and persevering in dealing with others.

The following summer I attended the Stress on Analytical Reasoning Program (SOAR) at Xavier University. Its purpose is to prepare incoming students for science and math courses. This program was the final determining factor in my becoming a Chemistry major at Xavier University.

Prior to entering Xavier, I became a volunteer worker at Louisiana State Medical School in New Orleans. As a result, I participated in research studies pertaining to cancer as an inherited disease. In addition, I actively participated in the growth of amniotic fluid cell cultures which helped me to learn the importance of cleanliness and sterile equipment.

At Xavier, I am a member of various social organizations and academic honor societies. At the end of my sophomore year, a decision was made to become less involved in extracurricular activities and to focus my energies on my courses. As a result, I completed the junior year, my hardest year as a Chemistry major, even more motivated than before. The science courses that I have taken left me fascinated with the structure and systems of the human body. I wish to continue my quest for knowledge in medical school, to further my understanding of how the body functions.

While attending Xavier, I also held a job as a student lab assistant in the hematology department of Charity Hospital in New Orleans. For two years I worked approximately twenty-five hours a week and became very familiar with the operations of this department. I tested blood for sickle cell anemia and learned how to do retic counts, but became most experienced in urinalysis. In addition, I was able to see how doctors are viewed by other hospital personnel.

Intrinsically, I am highly motivated. Extrinsically, I have a loving, supportive family and the confidence of the highly competent faculty of Xavier. Together, the above supply me with the confidence, courage and knowledge needed not only to attend medical school, but also to succeed. Having spent the last several years of life preparing to learn how to help the sick and the needy, I feel that my talents can best be exercised by becoming a doctor and working to heal others. This is my goal in life.

Essay #40

A s a child I believed that the answer to the polite old question of what I would like to do when I grow up was a simple one. One just chose what one did best, most naturally and loved the most. It seemed so easy to answer; I would grow up and help people. Although my basic approach had a lot of truth to it, my naivete of the complexities of decision-making is apparent. Knowledgeable decisions require more than just good instinct.

All the truly important resolutions in our lives require time and care. Benjamin Franklin used to sit and write out the pros and cons of each problem before arriving at a decision. He gave each reason a rating which he then tallied for an answer carrying the highest score. This process gave him the opportunity to identify the really weighty issues and allowed him to take the wisest course.

As a thoughtful individual I can appreciate Franklin's approach as I have come to live the pros and cons which have led me to my recent career decision. My desire to study medicine was born out of my attempts to understand and help people and my pursuit of the discipline of psychology.

I have studied many perspectives in psychology, and the more I learned the more I realized that the field had too narrow a focus on people. It really addressed only half the issue of human development by virtually ignoring the biological aspects of human behavior. Understanding the whole individual means learning about both the psychological and biological facets, since neither is complete without the other. Having recognized this vital link between the two fields, I have actively dedicated myself to pursuing a career that encompasses both disciplines.

I have never let go of my interest in people. To really excel and truly appreciate my career choice, I have held on to my youthful ideal of identifying with that special quality of helping people which comes so naturally to me. While some would be reluctant to change course, I have welcomed the challenge and allowed my experience in psychology to help me clearly define my goals. I, unfortunately, took chemistry at a time when it had little relevance in my life; psychology had consumed my interest. I missed most of the classes and should have dropped the course; a mistake that I hope is one of very few.

By taking the time to explore and better organize my skills, I have also been able to make a knowledgeable and intellectually sound decision.

E s s a y   # 4 1

S ome of my foremost objectives in the past three years have been to obtain a "well rounded" education, determine the benefits of a medical career, and to prepare myself adequately for such a career. By choosing a social science (economics) as a major and by working in research labs at the University of Minnesota (Minneapolis) Medical School during the past three summers, I believe I have attained all three goals. My transcript and recommendations attest to my progress in the first goal. In the remaining essay, I will comment on my progress in the latter two.

Having witnessed a limited sample of the routines of physicians at the University of Minnesota hospital during the past three summers, I think one of the greatest satisfactions of practicing medicine would be correctly diagnosing a patient, prescribing an effective treatment, and observing the patient's recovery. Moreover, a physician would be able to reap these benefits daily.

In the long run though, I would like to be a physician who researches medicine on a "basic science" level and, at the same time, translates advances in scientific theory into clinical practice. I have spent the past two summers working on projects which, at first, do not appear applicable to current medical problems, but may eventually help lead to new clinical treatments. For example, last summer I researched the effects of human fibrinogen on the phagocytosis of Escherichia coli by human polymorpho-nuclear neutrophils (PMNs). My study revealed that an indirect relation-ship exists between fibrinogen concentration and phagocytic killing by neutrophils. This conclusion might appear interesting but clinically of little value; it may, however, help elucidate the mechanism by which fibrin clots inhibit phagocytosis of E. coli by neutrophils. Hence, a treatment could be developed which might prevent the formation of peritoneal abscesses and intraabdominal sepsis. An accomplishment like this would be, I believe, of great and lasting satisfaction.

Presently, I am working on a project studying the effects of hyperoxia on cutaneous wounds. The literature reveals that when an inoculum of E. coli is injected intradermally with a mass inoculation gun into a guinea pig, the resultant lesion will be smaller if the animal is contained in a hyperoxic environment. The literature, so far, makes no reference to a mechanism. To identify this mechanism is the object of my current investigation.

The research hypothesis loosely reads, "increased partial pressures of oxygen in the ambient air lead to a more effective exidative burst on the part of the neutrophils; thus, bacteria are cleared from the wound more quickly, and the wound can heal faster." The practical applications of this project are more readily apparent than in my previous research. People with cutaneous wounds could be treated more effectively with the administration of oxygen. Again, an advancement in the understanding of a basic science problem, such as wound healing, would have been translated into clinical practice. Satisfactions such as this are one of my main reasons for choosing medicine.

E s s a y # 4 2

*P*raeludium. In the beginning there was dissonance. The lifeless world was still and silent. Then God breathed life unto man, giving realm of his own. And then one night, man was given the power to create, to discover and to question. And as he created fire to heal him from the cold, he discovered the sound of the flickers generated by his fire-maker. Like Apollo's Lyre when forged by Hermes, man's instrument was imbued with the magic of life. The magic to heal him from the cold he called medicine. The magic to create new sounds which brought him internal warmth he called music. Undoubtedly, music and medicine were born on the same day. From Apollo, who is god of both, to Johannes Brahms' best friend and trusted critic, the famous surgeon Theodore Billroth, music and medicine have courted each other incessantly. I am in love with both.

Allegro ma non troppo. My love for music is more than the desire to compose, interpret and listen; like my love for medicine is more than the desire to conduct research, practice and study. Rather, I wish to understand these two worlds, to internalize their principles so they become second nature to me, for love alone is not enough. I have not always felt this way: I decided to pursue medicine only after my second year in college. And music was not very exciting to me when I was sixteen. Unrelated yet similar incidents propelled me into these realms. I don't really know how it happened, but one day while playing the piano, I decided to improvise. As I played new combinations of notes, I felt free, uninhibited. Needless to say, my improvisations soon became compositions. Discovering that I could be original, treading on my own musical road was one of the greatest gifts of life, because it radically modified my approach to music. In medicine it happened differently. During my first 2 years in college I wished to become a biochemical researcher, but a key factor unknown to me was missing. During spring break I volunteered to do social work in a small Mexican village. With some romanticism I observed the village physician work with his rudimentary instrumentation healing, teaching and mainly learning in this isolated Shangri-La. Like with music, I learned that this physician could heal in his own creative way and be rich in spite of this town's emptiness. Doing this required creativity and openness. However, I made many mistakes after that because I asked what if I only compose? What if I study only medicine?

Andante. Soon after beginning to compose, my piano skills were weakened and I found myself lacking discipline. Eventually, my composition ceased because there was no knowledge on which to base my ideas. Similarly, I began to doubt my studies at Stanford. It seemed so much easier to return to Mexico where one begins medical school after high school. In music and medicine there exists a fine artistic domain which permits individual expression, care and much subjectivity. Yet this freedom can subsist because there is a rigid framework supporting and fueling it. To the composer this freedom is the realm of emotions. In the medical world this artistic domain is expressed in the individuality of each person. Often, even in what appears to be straight procedural medicine, one finds room for subjectivity. I once translated for a urologist with a Spanish-speaking patient. She had been preliminarily diagnosed with kidney stones and came to see a specialist. The urologist began with an interview rather than a physical. As he progressed he soon discovered that the patient's husband was abusing her both sexually and physically. No kidney stones were found and she was subsequently treated by a therapist. I was inspired by this physician's ability to seek alternate explanations, literally outside his area of expertise. But he was able to carry this freedom because his understanding of medicine is so complete, and so profound. So I decided to study harmony and develop a deeper understanding of music. It then became evident to me that Stanford was the right choice. Perhaps the common bond between music and medicine is their dual nature. There seems to be no clear border between the artistic and the scientific aspects of either. The famous composer Shoenberg once said that everything of supreme value in art must show "heart" as well as "brain." Perhaps this is the most important lesson I have learned: to use my subjective freedom better by strengthening its fundamental base. When I began my research on eating disorders I was given much freedom, being able to design studies entirely by myself. The only given was the issue to address. At that point I began to cherish the vast resources of the medical library, in strengthening my knowledge. In music, when I began to play the flute, I decided to focus on technique rather than feeling. And I have learned more about both in the last year than ever before. With the flute I have also discovered the joys of multi-instrumental music, chamber music. The ideal medical team should be like a chamber ensemble, each contributing to the whole, yet not drowning the others or becoming impersonal. I would like to practice thus.

165

Adagio. Important as music is to me, I have not considered music vocationally. Mainly for one reason: even though I love to perform and write music for others, music plays a selfish role in my life. It challenges my senses and intelligence, and often it heals me, yet I cannot offer my knowledge to others. Medicine offers me many of the same challenges and satisfactions that music does, yet throughout I know that I can act for others as well. This is vital to me. In the past few weeks I have suffered because of the earthquake in my Mexico City. That day, especially, there was no room for music, only for medicine, and I grieved for my lack of knowledge.

Allegro con spirite. Whenever I study a musical piece I study the biography of the composer. I believe that music always reflects the personality of the composer. Sometimes it reflects temporal feelings; others it reflects the composer's constant views on life. I choose to believe this because my music is entirely human. I write music for people, and sometimes write about people; but I always write as a human. In the same way I choose to believe that medicine is primarily human. It is very easy to lose track of this, especially while doing research, when one thinks in terms of enzymes and tRNA. I like to see both music and medicine in "Gestalt" terms. As I face my instrument, myriads of combinations flash across my mind and I visualize the harmonic implications of many, yet I cannot explain how I piece my notes together. Something deeper which I know not is ever-present in my style. In medical terms, I've observed this in Anorexia Nervosa. This disorder is treated by some with pure psychology, others treat it as a physiological sickness. Yet there's much more to it. On one level there exists social pressure, family problems etc.; but deeper there must be a physiological mechanism which operates concurrently with the rest. One world influences the other, resulting in a deadlocked circle. Subtle feelings which permeate my harmony, of the subtle biochemical processes that transcend the purely psychological; always knowing that this is life I am dealing with. Music and medicine have no lives of their own. Man gives them life so that they might celebrate his life. My flute lies before me, inorganic, not even latent. And yet I breathe life unto it and it speaks, sings, soothes. So lies my profession before me, and I can hardly wait to breathe life unto it so that it may in turn speak, sing, soothe and heal, breathing new life unto others.

Essay #43

S enior year at The Spence School, I discovered how interrelated the sciences could be. Understanding the basis of computer function and its similarities to the electrochemical nature of the nervous system, I realized how interesting the study of nature would be, especially with regards to the human system.

The summer following graduation I worked in the lab of Dr. P. R. Smith studying protein structure through electron microscopy. I was amazed how such research was based on basic principles within my grasp. I also began to realize how research on a day-to-day basis evolves rather than explodes, progressing by a series of smaller steps and variations on known procedures. The entire process seemed more like creative "playing" than work, despite the vast amount of knowledge behind each new variation. For two summers I worked in this lab developing a procedure to record electron micrographs of rotated crystals, making possible 3-D reconstruction of the protein.

The following two summers I worked for Dr. Robert D. Allen at the Marine Biological Laboratory in Woods Hole. Dr. Allen was a role model in both professional and personal aspects. In the lab Dr. Allen had perfected the art of "playing" with a specimen and allowed me free rein to do the same. It was here I learned the value of "playing" with a specimen (in educated ways) in order to obtain the desired result. Our attempts to disturb the microtubules in extruded axoplasm resulted in our paper on "gliding microtubules." Outside the lab Dr. Allen expressed his creativity in his cello performances. I began to see how deciphering a biological system was comparable to figuring out a "harmony." I also enjoy both listening to and performing music and hope to strike a rewarding balance between personal and professional creativity as Dr. Allen did.

The two summers I spent at MBL had a profound effect on my approach to my studies and instilled in me a desire to learn as much as possible. Surrounded by distinguished scientists and taking advantage of daily lectures, I came to realize that learning is a privilege. My ability to grasp difficult concepts improved with my increased exposure to new fields.

During these summers of research, however, I realized how important human interactions are to me. In high school I spent two years helping my grandmother through the difficulties associated with age. After she died, I enjoyed helping the elderly at holiday dinners organized by our church. In losing my closest grandparent, I gained several hundred more. In grade school my father sustained multiple heart attacks and during my sophomore year he suffered a stroke. The following year was made more difficult when both my aunt and Dr. Allen developed cancer. During this period I began to see how illness and medicine related to the sciences I had been studying, and I realized this was the field I was most interested in pursuing.

I returned to Amherst determined to put my knowledge into my senior research project. In order to devote myself totally to this goal, I decided to wait a year before applying to medical school. My experience with and love of photography played a major role in our success as my aesthetic sense and desire to get good photographs of beautiful cells constantly led us to better pictures and an abundance of cytological information we had not expected.

While I have participated in research over the last four years, I have seen its applications help my own family. I would therefore gain satisfaction from involvement in both the research aspect of medicine and its practical applications in patient care.

E s s a y # 4 4

*M*y goal for wanting to attend medical school is not to become just another M.D. but instead to become a warm and caring physician who is willing and able to humbly serve the people and their community to bring about improvements for the present human condition. In order to accomplish such a task, one must have the necessary dedication, knowledge and love for others.

Dedication to a worthy goal is important because this is what enables one to accomplish things beyond the ordinary limit. In whatever one does, without dedication, he can only reach mediocrity. This summer, through the help of the U.C.C. (United Church of Christ), I had the opportunity to dedicate my vacation to working as a volunteer at a missionary hospital in a small town called Humacao in Puerto Rico. While working there I've gained practical experience in different departments of the hospital. The most learning experience was working as a physician's assistant at their Home Care Program. In this program, health care professionals commute for hours to reach isolated households in the countryside to give treatment to those poor patients who cannot get to the hospital themselves. From working with these dedicated physicians I realized that a strong sense of dedication is the driving force that pushes one to achieve deeds that are beyond the limit of an ordinary doctor. That is why I want to become a humble, compassionate doctor who is sincerely dedicated to improving the human condition.

However, with dedication alone I cannot accomplish this task; I need the necessary skills and knowledge which will enable me to take actions toward my goal. During my years at Cornell, I've concentrated on getting a well-rounded liberal education rather than a science-oriented premedical education. I've tried to study as many courses in humanities and social sciences as I could, and I'm also majoring in Spanish literature because I believe one must first be a well-rounded human being who can think before he can become a competent worker in any field of profession. Knowledge is not knowing a lot of scientific facts and data, but instead it's the ability to think creatively and analytically, the power of observation and problem solving, and the infinite curiosity to discover the unknown. This year I'll be doing undergraduate research on lipid biochemistry because I believe that exploring into what is unknown is equally important as mastering what is already known. I want to become a kind of a doctor who will expand the horizon of the current medical knowledge because the never-ending desire to understand the inexplicable is the key to the progress of the world.

Dedication and knowledge are indispensable elements in the making of a warm and caring physician; however, they are not sufficient. In order to become a "complete" doctor who is competent, compassionate and understanding, one must be able to love mankind. In the future I want to become a loving doctor who has a warm, family-like relationship with each and every one of his patients, the kind of a doctor who can readily communicate and understand his patients on a one-to-one basis because such doctor-patient communication is invaluable in treating a patient. During my undergraduate years I've been involved in a wide range of extracurricular and community activities from which I've learned a lot about human relations. I've also worked overseas where I've been exposed to different people and culture. From these experiences I've gained the patience, understanding and a caring heart, all of which are necessary in communicating and dealing with all kinds of difficult people and situations, and I believe this qualification will help me greatly in becoming a compassionate and understanding doctor who can readily meet the needs of the people.

E s s a y # 4 5

*M*y desire to become a physician originated during my childhood, a time when my father, who is himself a physician, served as my primary mentor and role model. As I matured, the initially blind longings he instilled in me were transformed into apprised aspirations and viable expectations. I have come to esteem medicine as a dynamic field promising a career filled with challenge and change. In addition, it offers the opportunity to have a positive impact on society while insuring a measure of respect and financial security. Equally appealing to me are medicine's clinical aspects, for I greatly value the chance to interact with a varying mix of people in diverse situations.

That these elements are indeed important career expectations for me has been self-substantiated by numerous personal experiences. Growing up in a family of seven, I have known all my life the pleasures of cooperation and inter-human relationships. In addition, my many years of participation in team sports have increased my proclivity for group interaction, as have my more recent experiences living with twenty other individuals in my fraternity house. This need for close contact and association with people has always been a prominent facet of my personality, and it is one I hope will find continued expression through clinical medicine.

I have also always felt the need to be challenged, and this has afforded me some very gratifying experiences. Entering college I had no prior exposure to secure myself a spot in the Crew program. This led to two very enjoyable seasons of rowing, and allowed me to develop some close friendships in addition to the techniques and skills of a new sport. Sportscasting was also foreign to me prior to college, but over the past three years I have managed to work my way up to the senior position among hockey commentators at the college radio station. This pursuit has not only proved to be exciting, but also quite beneficial as it has improved my extemporaneous oratory skills.

I have also tried to challenge myself academically at college, and this pledge bolstered my resolution to undertake study of the Chinese language. While these have perhaps been my most difficult courses, they have also been my most enjoyable. From them I have developed a fascination with the Chinese culture which not only has led me to major in this area, but, beginning this summer, I will undertake an intensive three month course of study in the People's Republic of China, followed by an additional three months of study in Taiwan. It is my hope that these next six months will not only afford me fluency in the Chinese language, but an intimate look at an alien culture and the opportunity to augment my intellectual and emotional growth, as well.

Though limited by space, it is my hope that these few preceding examples demonstrate my commitment to the characteristics of a career in medicine. Furthermore, I have strengthened this commitment through extensive service as a hospital volunteer. Since high school I have worked at different hospitals in patient transport, intensive care, and pediatrics. My current volunteer work playing with hospitalized children typifies the whole range of these experiences. The immediate emotional gratification I receive from my work, though tempered by an often brutal reality, has made my attraction towards medicine even more genuine and concrete.

As I conclude, a Confucian aphorism comes to mind: "The wise embrace all knowledge, but they are most earnest about what is of the greatest importance." Throughout college I have been diligent in embracing many different streams of knowledge. However, graduation necessitates an estimation of these varied intellectual pursuits, and, for me, there is little question that, among them, my ambition to study medicine ranks supreme.

E s s a y # 4 6

"If you don't get paid, why the hell do you work here?" While working at the Pine Street Inn, Boston's largest shelter for the homeless, this question came up often. Before giving an honest answer, one is forced to do a lot of soul-searching. I could have, after all, chosen a more pleasant placement than the Inn, where for ten hours a week I comforted and assisted hundreds of alcoholic and often deeply disturbed individuals. These derelicts shared a misery too profound for words.

In such an atmosphere of despair and frustration, one must still try to find some achievement for your own piece of mind, while dealing with a social system that has completely failed these individuals. The Inn teaches you to strive for improvement no matter how small, and even though so much is needed. In trying your best at whatever you do, it is important to understand your own limitations, both personal and within the system. Several times I've spent hours talking to a "guest," and have left the Inn beaming with a sense of accomplishment only to be discouraged when a week later my new friend is on the floor, quiet in unconsciousness except for an occasional cough from lungs that only God could have designed to last through such punishment. Compassion is born in places like this, and can possess you totally if not kept in perspective.

A physician's practice in many ways parallels this experience. His limitations are the scientific laws governing our bodies. When fighting for another's life becomes your vocation, losing to death becomes a hard pill to swallow. Our knowledge of medicine is ever-growing, yet the nemesis of death will always be the final victor.

Why ride an emotional rollercoaster and volunteer at the Pine Street Inn, or dedicate yourself to becoming a physician? Because in helping people, you gain an understanding and compassion that sensitizes you to a wide range of human conditions, and makes you want to do your share in trying to better them.

Essay #47

I was born in Hungary and received a well-rounded education complete with 10 years of extracurricular piano, singing, ballet and language lessons. From an early age I was fascinated by the scientific and technological advances of the West to the extent that I decided to emigrate and, at the age of 12, began to study English in preparation for this move. I received a Ph.D. in Psychobiology from Eotvos Lorand University in Budapest and left for the U.S.A. the same year.

I received a postdoctoral fellowship at the Neurology Department of the University of Pennsylvania Medical School. Here I learned about various brain imaging techniques such as Positron Emission Tomography (PET), Nuclear Magnetic Resonance and regional Cerebral Blood Flow and developed a strong interest in functional neuroanatomy. I devised a PET study which demonstrated an asymmetry of glucose metabolism in the human posterior parietal lobes during the performance of directed attentional tasks. Furthermore, I demonstrated an asymmetry of cortical control of heart rate in humans under conditions of unilateral barbituration of the hemispheres. Neither of the above had been previously reported in the literature. I was also involved in projects studying the impact of cognitive tasks on cerebral glucose metabolism, glucose metabolism changes in epilepsy and in schizophrenia.

I was invited to present my findings at Behavioral Neurology Grand Rounds at Beth Israel Hospital of Harvard Medical School and was offered a two-year NIH institutional National Research Service Award. At Harvard I worked on a study describing the distribution of acetylocholinesteraze in the primate cortex and a study describing the cortico-cortical connectivity of the temporal poles of primates. I also had the opportunity to attend Neurology Grand Rounds and Behavioral Neurology Grand Rounds on a weekly basis for 2 years. This experience was my first exposure to brain-lesioned patients and it made me realize that clinical observation is perhaps the richest source of information in the study of neuroanatomical correlates of human behavior. I found the clinical experience intellectually fascinating as well as emotionally stimulating and it triggered a strong desire in me to become a physician.

Two years ago I enrolled in the post-baccalaureate premedical program of Hunter College. Last year I had the singular honor of being placed at the top of the list of accepted candidates at both the Cornell and Mount Sinai Medical School linkage programs. I have chosen the Cornell program due to its PET facility as well as its exceptional reputation in the neurosciences.

My mother swears that I kept mumbling "Dad is dead" in a
sickening mantra as we ran up the dark, wet road late on that
cold summer's night. I don't recall saying it at all, as I was
much younger, but the sight of my mother running frantically past me is
forever etched in my memory. My father is not dead, by the way, although
the accident changed him forever.

Each August, my mother converts a children's sleep-away camp (after
the campers have gone home) into a week-long Israeli folk dance fantasy
camp for adults. That summer was its inaugural year. My family, several
friends, and I went to the camp the night before to ready it for the dancers
due to arrive the following day. Our preparations ranged from setting up a
colossal sound system to cleaning bunks. We wanted to ensure that all of
the little things that make an experience memorable were in order. My dad
considered it imperative that we decorate the gray sheet metal walled gym,
because no one would want to travel half the world to feel as though he
were a dancing sardine.

We borrowed a 25-foot ladder so that we could reach the ceiling to
hang our banners. The first few, which seemed enormous when we made
them in our basement, went up without a hitch and were dwarfed by the
monstrous walls. My father moved the ladder and hung the first corner of
the ill-fated decoration. He then repositioned and ascended the ladder to
hang the second corner. He paused for a second at the top when suddenly
the ladder slid across the polished gym floor. They both hurtled rapidly
downward as my dad held on tightly. Time was suspended as they fell. It
started again as my dad hit the floor, his body above the ladder, his arms
crushed below it and his head slamming against the floor with a heart
stopping thud. We all stood transfixed until the violent crashing noise of
the falling decoration propelled us back into reality. In an instant my mom
and I bolted up the dark, unfamiliar camp road to summon the camp nurse
from the infirmary. In retrospect, he may have looked dead just lying
there, but I really don't remember thinking or saying so as we ran. When
the nurse finally arrived, my mother fainted and both my parents wound up
in the hospital.

Despite the accident, there was still much preparation that had to be
done. The burden fell upon each of us still in the gym. With spirits
dampened and composure regained, we set back to work.

At the hospital, my father received several doses of Demerol to ease the pain of two broken elbows, a shattered wrist, and a broken nose. In between lapses of concentration and nods of sleep, my dad explained to my technologically impaired mother how to set up the sound equipment and its labyrinth of wires. My mom nervously and patiently transcribed every word and returned to the camp. Much to her chagrin, her friends had spent the night piecing the system together. After a careful comparison with her notes, she began to cry. Although it was functional, they did it "wrong." Her friends, acting with a rare and humbling compassion, proceeded to dismantle their entire night's work and tried to reassemble the system according to my drug-impaired father's specifications. I was awed by the empathy and understanding they showed.

The camp that year became a gathering of dancers from five continents and was an astounding success. It has since become the largest dance camp of its type in the world. My mother tells us that my father's tenacious spirit and his "show must go on" perseverance has been passed down like a precious heirloom. She has seen these same traits in my brothers and me since we were young children. I can now see them developing in my younger sister.

My dad's fall had no direct bearing on my decision to study medicine. However, it made me realize how strong my desire to be a doctor really was. The events that night triggered feelings of inadequacy within me. "I will be a doctor someday," I thought. "Why can't that day be today so I can help him?"

I vividly recall that I was overcome by a sense of urgency. It subsided as my energies focused on achieving that goal. In its place remained an unwavering commitment, fervor and passion to practice medicine.

The sense of urgency still emerges occasionally when a severely injured person is wheeled into the hospital emergency room where I volunteer. I am reminded of my father's fall. Fortunately, my determination to be a doctor quickly takes control as I observe the frenzied calm of the ER team bringing healing to the sick. My passionate commitment to pursue medicine is reaffirmed.

Essay #49

*T*hough I would not wish it on anyone else, my experience as an asthmatic has ingrained in me poignant memories of being a patient. Those episodes have always served as my motivation for a career in medicine. I recently watched a show on the Discovery Channel about a real life day in the ER. A young child with a wire stuck in his throat was calmed by the attending doctors who then removed the wire. The child had been pretending it was a microphone because he wanted to be a singer. Later that day, when asked if he still wanted to be a singer, the child said, "No, I want to be a doctor." I truly understand that. The memories of the fine medical staff who helped me throughout my life are a large factor in choosing medicine to be my life's work. Along with the empathy of a patient, however, is a love of science. Majoring in biology, attending seminars, and conducting ongoing research made it clear that medicine is the way to marry my love of science with my desire to continually challenge myself and work with others. Would I have come to the same conclusion if I had been a totally healthy child? Perhaps, but the unique crossroads where I now find myself is the result of a path I started on many years ago, and what I have to offer as a physician is the culmination of my life's worth of experiences.

By the time I was 13, I had been through numerous severe asthma attacks. After nine years of allergy shots, my condition had improved significantly. However, the surprise attack that landed me in the emergency room that year prompted my allergist to retest me. He found that I had developed a sensitivity to dust mites as extreme as he had ever seen. At that point, in the face of this setback, I became determined to deal with my asthma, conquer it, and never let it stop me from doing what I wanted. That dedication and perseverance has never left me. I do not leave things half done, and my efforts are never token ones. When I set my mind to accomplishing a task, no obstacle can deter me.

In my sophomore year of college, I became involved in the designing of a web page for the introductory Microbiology class. I developed a proposal that earned a grant from the American Society of Microbiology (ASM). I then set about learning the hypertext markup language that is used to design pages on the Internet. With no previous experience, I was able to not only learn the language but also complete the web page project from start to finish. The quality of the finished web page was such that ASM awarded me a travel grant and the opportunity to give an oral presentation at the annual conference held in Atlanta. Concurrently, I was, and continue to be, involved in laboratory research geared towards developing a sensitive diagnostic test for the detection of pathogenic Cryptosporidium oocyst. The many long hours I have spent in the laboratory running countless experiments have further heightened my understanding of the words perseverance and dedication. I understand that becoming a doctor will require spending long hours, learning daunting amounts of information, and passing challenging tests. I believe my determination and dedication will serve me well.

I also feel that I have much to offer in terms of patient interaction. Patients are people who are sick, and, perhaps more importantly, scared. I remember many times going to my allergist's office in the midst of a severe asthma attack. I was a scared little boy who could not breathe. His gentle demeanor, soothing tone of voice, and sense of humor all served to put me at ease. With this in mind, I have taken and excelled in a class on Oral Communication. Furthermore, the significance of a sense of humor has not been lost on me. At Cornell, I have been in theatrical productions and auditioned for and become part of an improvisational comedy group. I especially enjoy the comedy group because it affords me the opportunity to do one of the things I love to do most—make someone laugh. The soup kitchen where I volunteered was also unique in that it afforded me a chance not only to cook, serve, and clean up, but also to eat and interact with the clients. One night, I remember speaking with an unhappy young woman. I told her a story which amused her, she began to laugh in spite of herself, and her mood immediately changed. That I could make her laugh made me proud. I believe my sense of humor is one of my greatest assets.

Mine is a charmed life. In it, I have been blessed many times: a loving family, good friends, and asthma. While not many people view a debilitating childhood affliction as an asset, in retrospect, I can see that it was for me. In the end, I guess a pair of over-reactive bronchioles were not all that bad.

E s s a y   # 5 0

I worked in the observatory this summer as a computer programmer. Working in programming was a valuable learning experience but even more valuable was observing the interaction between people in the maintenance staff, the technical staff, and the scientific staff. It was often interesting to see how important was all their work to keep the observatory running smoothly. I will relate what I observed during one of my days of work.

This day was very important for one of the scientists. After about five to six years of planning an experiment, the day for performing the experiment had arrived. The experiment was done in conjunction with the Space Shuttle. At about midnight, the Shuttle would boost its engines right above the radio-telescope; gasses from the engines would disturb the ionosphere, making a hole in it. This disturbance would be observed from the telescope for about twelve hours.

By 11:00pm the experimenter had all the equipment ready to observe the hole. The only missing information was the exact coordinates at which the Shuttle would burn the ionosphere, and this information would be given in a phone call from Houston at about 11:45pm.

At about 11:30pm a technician repairing a phone line damaged by a thunderstorm accidentally turned on a switch that caused a shutdown of all phone communications. The closest phone to the observatory is about half an hour away by car. The atmosphere in the observatory was tense. Some other workers were teasing the technician while he tried to recover the communication lines. They were telling him that due to his blunder the experiment would fail. The experimenter was nervous; the technician was even more nervous.

Sometime around 11:50pm the technician fixed the line, communication with Houston was possible, and the experimenter received the coordinates. The data was collected and everything looked as if it was all right.

I realized afterwards that nothing of what I related here will be known to someone looking at a research paper on this experiment. A lot of the work done by the maintenance employees, the technicians, and the scientists remains hidden and unrecognized by someone just looking at the results. But all this work is important and essential to the progress of research.

Also unnoticed remain the human qualities of all these personnel, which in a given circumstance may affect the outcome of their joint endeavor. In my example, the worker's response of enjoying the technician's misfortune could have impaired his ability to fix the line quickly. In other instances workers were extremely helpful to one another, and better than usual working situations were created. Whenever human beings interact, human qualities will show up, some favorable and some unfavorable, and in the same way that they could affect the result of an experiment they could also have an effect in other fields of work.

EPILOGUE

*M*edicine is not only an applied science, it is also an art, and the art of medicine lies in the healer's insight, empathy, and ability to communicate with the patient effectively. Young physicians must enter medicine compassionate and dedicated to a professional calling.

We stress these essential qualities because, all to often, people who could be great physicians get discouraged from applying to medical school. If you have a sincere interest in serving the sick, don't underestimate your fitness for medicine. A low grade point average or mediocre MCAT scores should not dissuade you from becoming a physician.

Follow the formula we have outlined, have a positive outlook toward medicine and the admissions process, persevere, and you will be offered an acceptance to a medical school. Do your best—no one can ask for more. Remember, top-notch applicants with the proper outlook and personality are always in high demand.

The bureaucracy and stress involved in the admissions process may cloud your original goal and diminish your desire. Don't let yourself get disillusioned and discouraged, and be patient. In time, you will be practicing medicine, and you will be in a position to really help others.

> *Destiny is not a matter of chance, it's a matter of choice. It's not something to be waited for, it's something to be achieved.*
>
> *—Robert Browning*

We recall vividly the hassle of marketing ourselves and the anxiety we felt during the admissions process. Writing the essay, completing applications on time, buying the appropriate clothes to project the proper image, sweating during the interview, checking the mailbox several times a day for an acceptance/rejection letter— it's all part of the rites of passage to medicine. Repeatedly, we would ask, "Is it really worth it?"

Well, now we can honestly answer: yes. There is always something new to learn about disease, injury, patients, and even yourself. Medicine becomes a philosophy that assigns meaning and purpose to our society. Most significant, there is no greater feeling than knowing that every day as a doctor you are able to make a difference in the life of another.

We wish you the best of luck in your career. You have made it this far, and taking the initiative to read this book shows you are heading in the right direction. Have confidence in yourself and your accomplishments, and one day you *will* become a physician!

ABOUT THE AUTHORS

John A. Zebala received his M.D. and Ph.D. from Cornell University as a W.H. Keck Foundation Fellow and graduated with a B.S. in Biomedical Engineering from the University of Southern California. He completed specialty training in Laboratory Medicine and Anatomic Pathology at the University of Washington. Dr. Zebala is currently the President and CEO of Syntrix Biochip, a technology company he founded in Seattle.

Daniel B. Jones is an Assistant Professor of Surgery at University of Texas Southwestern Medical Center and Director of the Southwestern Center for Minimally Invasive Surgery (www.swmed.edu/cmis). He attended undergraduate and medical school at Cornell University. He completed surgery residency and a fellowship in laparoscopy at Washington University School of Medicine in St. Louis.

Stephanie B. Jones graduated from Washington University School of Medicine and completed her training in anesthesiology at Barnes-Jewish Hospital in St. Louis. She is currently an Assistant Professor in the Department of Anesthesiology and Pain Management at University of Texas Southwestern Medical Center at Dallas.

Directory of U.S. Medical Schools

The following is a list of the addresses and phone numbers of medical schools in the United States. Below each address is information regarding AMCAS status (see Chapter 4), the application deadline, and the public/private status of the school.

Alabama
Univ. of Alabama School of Medicine
Office of Medical Student Svcs/Admissions
VH100
Birmingham, AL 35294-0019
(205) 934-2330
AMCAS • Deadline: Nov 1 • Public

Univ. of S. Alabama College of Medicine
Office of Admissions, 2015 MSB
Mobile, AL 36688-0002
(334) 460-7176
AMCAS • Deadline: Nov 15 • Public

Arizona
Univ. of Arizona College of Medicine
Admissions Office, Room 2209
Tucson, AZ 85724-5075
(520) 626-6214
AMCAS • Deadline: Nov 1 • Public

Arkansas
Univ. of Arkansas College of Medicine
Office of Student Admissions, Slot 551
4301 West Markham Street
Little Rock, AR 72205-7199
(501) 686-5354
AMCAS • Deadline: Nov 1 • Public

California
Univ. of California—Davis
School of Medicine Admissions Office
Davis, CA 95616
(916) 752-2717
AMCAS • Deadline: Nov 1 • Public

Univ. of California—Irvine
College of Medicine
P.O. Box 4089
Medical Education Building
Irvine, CA 92717
(800) 824-5388
AMCAS • Deadline: Nov 1 • Public

University of California—Los Angeles
School of Medicine
Office of Student Affairs/Div. of Admissions
Center for Health Sciences
Los Angeles, CA 90095-1720
(310) 825-6081
AMCAS • Deadline: Nov 1 • Public

Drew/UCLA Joint Medical Program
Drew Univ. of Medicine and Science
1621 East 120th Street
Los Angeles, CA 90059
(213) 563-4952
AMCAS • Deadline: Nov 15 • Public

Univ. of California—San Diego
School of Medicine
Office of Admissions, 0621
Medical Teaching Facility
9500 Gilman Drive
La Jolla, CA 92093-0621
(619) 534-3880
AMCAS • Deadline: Nov 1 • Public

Univ. of California—San Francisco
School of Medicine
Admissions, C-200, Box 0408
San Francisco, CA 94143
(415) 476-4044
AMCAS • Deadline: Nov 1 • Public

Loma Linda Univ. School of Medicine
Associate Dean for Admissions
Loma Linda, CA 92350
(909) 824-4467
AMCAS • Deadline: Nov 15 • Private

Univ. of Southern California School of Medicine
Office of Admissions
1975 Zonal Avenue
Los Angeles, CA 90033
(213) 342-2552
AMCAS • Deadline: Nov 1 • Private

Stanford Univ. School of Medicine
Office of Admissions
851 Welch Road, Room 154
Palo Alto, CA 94304-1677
(650) 723-6861
AMCAS • Deadline: Nov 1 • Private

Colorado
Univ. of Colorado School of Medicine
Medical School Admissions
4200 East 9th Avenue, C-297
Denver, CO 80262
(303) 315-7361
AMCAS • Deadline: Nov 15 • Public

Connecticut

Univ. of Connecticut School of Medicine
Office of Admissions and Student Affairs
263 Farmington Avenue, Room AG-062
Farmington, CT 06030-1905
(203) 679-2152
AMCAS • Deadline: Dec 15 • Public

Yale Univ. School of Medicine
Office of Admissions
367 Cedar Street
New Haven, CT 06510
(860) 785-2696
Deadline: Oct 15 • Private

District of Columbia

George Washington Univ. School of Medicine
Office of Admissions
2300 I Street NW, Room 615
Washington, DC 20037
(202) 994-3506
AMCAS • Deadline: Dec 1 • Private

Georgetown Univ. School of Medicine
Office of Admissions
3900 Reservoir Road, NW
Washington, DC 20007
(202) 687-1154
AMCAS • Deadline: Nov 1 • Private

Howard Univ. College of Medicine
Admissions Office
520 W Street, NW
Washington, DC 20059
(202) 806-6270
AMCAS • Deadline: Dec 15 • Private

Florida

Florida State Univ.
Program in Medical Sciences
Tallahassee, FL 32306-4051
(850) 644-1855
AMCAS • Deadline: Dec 15 • Public

Univ. of Florida College of Medicine
Chair, Medical Selection Committee
J. Hillis Miller Health Center
Gainesville, FL 32610
(904) 392-4569
AMCAS • Deadline: Dec 1 • Public

Univ. of Miami School of Medicine
Office of Admissions
P.O. Box 016159
Miami, FL 33101
(305) 547-6791
AMCAS • Deadline: Dec 1 • Private

Univ. of South Florida College of Medicine
Office of Admissions, Box 3
12901 Bruce B. Downs Blvd.
Tampa, FL 33612-4799
(813) 974-2229
AMCAS • Deadline: Dec 1 • Public

Georgia

Emory Univ. School of Medicine
Woodruff Health Sciences Center
Administration Bldg., Admissions, Room 303
Atlanta, GA 30322-4510
(404) 727-5660
AMCAS • Deadline: Oct 15 • Private

Medical College of Georgia School of Medicine
Associate Dean for Admissions
Augusta, GA 30912-4760
(706) 721-3186
AMCAS • Deadline: Nov 1 • Public

Mercer Univ. School of Medicine
Office of Admissions and Student Affairs
Macon, GA 31207
(912) 752-2542
AMCAS • Deadline: Dec 1 • Private

Morehouse School of Medicine
Admissions and Student Affairs
720 Westview Drive, SW
Atlanta, GA 30310-1495
(404) 752-1650
AMCAS • Deadline: Dec 1 • Private

Hawaii

Univ. of Hawaii Burns School of Medicine
Office of Admissions
1960 East-West Road
Honolulu, HI 96822
(808) 956-8300
AMCAS • Deadline: Dec 1 • Public

Illinois

Univ. of Chicago Pritzker School of Medicine
Office of the Dean of Students
924 East 57th Street, BLSC 104
Chicago, IL 60637
(773) 702-1939
AMCAS • Deadline: Nov 15 • Private

Finch Univ. of Health Sciences/
Chicago Medical School
Office of Admissions
3333 Green Bay Road
North Chicago, IL 60064
(847) 578-3205
AMCAS • Deadline: Dec 15 • Private

Univ. of Illinois College of Medicine
Office of Medical College Admissions
Room 165 CME MIC 783
808 South Wood Street
Chicago, IL 60612-7302
(312) 996-5635
AMCAS • Deadline: Dec 15 • Public

Loyola Univ. of Chicago
Stritch School of Medicine
Office of Admissions, Room 1752
2160 South First Avenue
Maywood, IL 60153
(708) 216-3229
AMCAS • Deadline: Nov 15 • Private

Northwestern Univ. Medical School
Associate Dean for Admissions
303 East Chicago Avenue
Chicago, IL 60611
(312) 503-8206
AMCAS • Deadline: Oct 15 • Private

Rush Medical College
Office of Admissions
524 Academic Facility
600 South Paulina Street
Chicago, IL 60612
(312) 942-6913
AMCAS • Deadline: Nov 15 • Private

Southern Illinois Univ. School of Medicine
Office of Student and Alumni Affairs
P.O. Box 19230
Springfield, IL 62794-9230
(217) 524-0326
AMCAS • Deadline: Nov 15 • Public

Indiana
Indiana Univ. School of Medicine
Medical School Admissions Office
Fesler Hall 213
1120 South Drive
Indianapolis, IN 46202-5113
(317) 274-3772
AMCAS • Deadline: Dec 15 • Public

Iowa
Univ. of Iowa College of Medicine
Director of Admissions
100 Medicine Administration Building
Iowa City, IA 52242-1101
(319) 335-8052
AMCAS • Deadline: Nov 1 • Public

Kansas
Univ. of Kansas School of Medicine
Associate Dean for Admissions
3901 Rainbow Blvd.
Kansas City, KS 66160-7301
(913) 588-5245
AMCAS • Deadline: Oct 15 • Public

Kentucky
Univ. of Kentucky College of Medicine
Admissions, Room MN-102, Office of Education
Chandler Medical Center
800 Rose Street
Lexington, KY 40536-0084
(606) 323-6161
AMCAS • Deadline: Nov 1 • Public

Univ. of Louisville School of Medicine
Office of Admissions
Health Sciences Center
Louisville, KY 40292
(502) 852-5193
AMCAS • Deadline: Nov 1 • Public

Louisiana
LSU-New Orleans School of Medicine
Admissions Office
1901 Perdido Street, Box P3-4
New Orleans, LA 70112-1393
(504) 568-6262
AMCAS • Deadline: Nov 15 • Public

LSU-Shreveport School of Medicine
Office of Student Admissions
P.O. Box 33932
Shreveport, LA 71130-3932
(318) 675-5190
AMCAS • Deadline: Nov 15 • Public

Tulane Univ. School of Medicine
Office of Admissions
1430 Tulane Ave, SL67
New Orleans, LA 70112-2699
(504) 588-5187
AMCAS • Deadline: Dec 15 • Private

Maryland
Johns Hopkins Univ. School of Medicine
Committee on Admission
720 Rutland Avenue
Baltimore, MD 21205-2196
(410) 955-3182
Deadline: Nov 1 • Private

Univ. of Maryland School of Medicine
Committee on Admissions, Room 1-005
655 West Baltimore Street
Baltimore, MD 21201
(410) 706-7478
AMCAS • Deadline: Nov 1 • Public

Uniformed Services U. of the Health Sciences
F. Edward Hebert School of Medicine
Admissions Office, Room A-1041
4301 Jones Bridge Road
Bethesda, MD 20814-4799
(800) 772-1743
AMCAS • Deadline: Nov 1 • Federally-chartered

Massachusetts

Boston Univ. School of Medicine
Admissions Office
Building L, Room 124
80 East Concord Street
Boston, MA 02118
(617) 638-4630
AMCAS • Deadline: Nov 15 • Private

Harvard Medical School
Office of Admissions
25 Shattuck Street
Boston, MA 02115-6092
(617) 432-1550
AMCAS • Deadline: Oct 15 • Private

Univ. of Massachusetts Medical School
Associate Dean for Admissions
55 Lake Avenue, North
Worcester, MA 01655
(508) 856-2323
AMCAS • Deadline: Nov 1 • Public

Tufts Univ. School of Medicine
Office of Admissions
136 Harrison Avenue
Boston, MA 02111
(617) 636-6571
AMCAS • Deadline: Nov 1 • Private

Michigan

Univ. of Michigan Medical School
Admissions Office
M4130 Medical Sciences I Building
Ann Arbor, MI 48109-0611
(734) 764-6317
AMCAS • Deadline: Nov 15 • Public

Michigan State U.. College of Human Medicine
Office of Admissions
A-239 Life Sciences
East Lansing, MI 48824-1317
(517) 353-9620
AMCAS • Deadline: Nov 15 • Public

Wayne State Univ. School of Medicine
Director of Admissions
540 East Canfield
Detroit, MI 48201
(313) 577-1466
AMCAS • Deadline: Dec 15 • Public

Minnesota

Mayo Medical School
Admissions Committee
200 First Street, SW
Rochester, MN 55905
(507) 284-3671
AMCAS • Deadline: Nov 1 • Private

Univ. of Minnesota-Duluth School of Medicine
Office of Admissions, Room 107
10 Univ. Drive
Duluth, MN 55812
(218) 726-8511
AMCAS • Deadline: Nov 15 • Public

Univ. of Minnesota Medical School
Office of Admissions and Student Affairs
Box 293-UMHC
420 Delaware Street, SE
Minneapolis, MN 55455-0310
(612) 624-1122
AMCAS • Deadline: Nov 15 • Public

Mississippi

Univ. of Mississippi School of Medicine
Chair, Admissions Committee
2500 North State Street
Jackson, MS 39216-4505
(601) 984-5010
AMCAS • Deadline: Nov 1 • Public

Missouri

Univ. of Missouri-Columbia School of Medicine
Office of Admissions
MA202 Medical Sciences Bldg.
One Hospital Drive
Columbia, MO 65212
(314) 882-2923
AMCAS • Deadline: Nov 1 • Public

U. of Missouri-Kansas City School of Medicine
Council on Selection
2411 Holmes
Kansas City, MO 64108
(816) 235-1870
Deadline: Nov 15 • Public

St. Louis Univ. School of Medicine
Admissions Committee
1402 South Grand Blvd.
St. Louis, MO 63104
(314) 577-8205
AMCAS • Deadline: Dec 15 • Private

Washington Univ. School of Medicine
Office of Admissions
660 South Euclid Avenue, #8107
St. Louis, MO 63110
(314) 362-6857
AMCAS • Deadline: Nov 15 • Private

Nebraska

Creighton Univ. School of Medicine
Office of Admissions
2500 California Plaza
Omaha, NE 68178
(402) 280-2798
AMCAS • Deadline: Dec 1 • Private

Univ. of Nebraska College of Medicine
Office of the Dean—Admissions
Wittson Hall Room 5017A
600 South 42nd Street
Omaha, NE 68198-6585
(402) 559-6140
AMCAS • Deadline: Nov 1 • Public

Nevada
Univ. of Nevada School of Medicine
Office of Admissions and Student Affairs
Mail Stop 357
Reno, NV 89557
(702) 784-6063
AMCAS • Deadline: Nov 1 • Public

New Hampshire
Dartmouth Medical School
Admissions
7020 Remsen, Room 306
Hanover, NH 03755-3833
(603) 650-1505
AMCAS • Deadline: Nov 1 • Private

New Jersey
UMDNJ—New Jersey Medical School
Director of Admissions
185 South Orange Avenue
Newark, NJ 07103
(973) 972-4631
AMCAS • Deadline: Dec 15 • Public

UMDNJ—R.W. Johnson Medical School
Office of Admissions
675 Hoes Lane
Piscataway, NJ 08854-5635
(908) 235-4576
AMCAS • Deadline: Dec 1 • Public

New Mexico
Univ. of New Mexico School of Medicine
Office of Admissions and Student Affairs
Basic Medical Sciences Building, Room 107
Albuquerque, NM 87131-5166
(505) 272-4766
AMCAS • Deadline: Nov 15 • Public

New York
Albany Medical College
Office of Admissions, A-3
47 New Scotland Avenue
Albany, NY 12208
(518) 262-5521
AMCAS • Deadline: Nov 15 • Private

Albert Einstein College of Medicine
Office of Admissions
Jack and Pearl Resnick Campus
1300 Morris Park Avenue
Bronx, NY 10461
(718) 430-2106
AMCAS • Deadline: Nov 1 • Private

Columbia U. College of Physicians & Surgeons
Admissions Office, Room 1-416
630 West 168th Street
New York, NY 10032
(212) 305-3595
Deadline: Oct 15 • Private

Cornell Univ. Medical College
Office of Admissions
445 East 69th Street
New York, NY 10021
(212) 746-1067
AMCAS • Deadline: Oct 15 • Private

Mount Sinai School of Medicine
Director of Admissions
Annenberg Bldg., Room 5-04
One Gustave L. Levy Place, Box 1002
New York, NY 10029-6574
(212) 241-6696
AMCAS • Deadline: Nov 1 • Private

New York Medical College
Office of Admissions
Room 127, Sunshine Cottage
Valhalla, NY 10595
(914) 594-4507
AMCAS • Deadline: Dec 1 • Private

New York Univ. School of Medicine
Office of Admissions
P.O. Box 1924
New York, NY 10016
(212) 263-5290
Deadline: Dec 1 • Private

U. of Rochester School of Medicine & Dentistry
Director of Admissions
Medical Center Box 601
Rochester, NY 14642
(716) 275-4539
AMCAS • Deadline: Oct 15 • Private

SUNY Brooklyn College of Medicine
Director of Admissions
450 Clarkson Avenue, Box 60M
Brooklyn, NY 11203
(718) 270-2446
AMCAS • Deadline: Dec 15 • Public

Univ. at Buffalo School of Medicine
Office of Medical Admissions
40 Biomedical Education Building
Buffalo, NY 14214-3013
(716) 829-3465
AMCAS • Deadline: Oct 15 • Public

SUNY Stony Brook School of Medicine
Health Sciences Center
Committee on Admissions/Level 4, Room 147
Stony Brook, NY 11794-8434
(516) 444-2113
AMCAS • Deadline: Nov 15 • Public

SUNY Syracuse College of Medicine
Admissions Committee
155 Elizabeth Blackwell Street
Syracuse, NY 13210
(315) 464-4570
AMCAS · Deadline: Nov 1 · Public

North Carolina
Wake Forest Univ. School of Medicine
Office of Medical School Admissions
Medical Center Blvd.
Winston-Salem, NC 27157-1090
(910) 716-4264
AMCAS · Deadline: Nov 1 · Private

Duke Univ. School of Medicine
Committee on Admissions
P.O. Box 3710
Durham, NC 27710
(919) 684-2985
AMCAS · Deadline: Oct 15 · Private

East Carolina Univ. School of Medicine
Assistant Dean, Office of Admissions
Greenville, NC 27858-4354
(919) 816-2202
AMCAS · Deadline: Nov 15 · Public

UNC Chapel Hill School of Medicine
Admissions Office
CB# 7000 MacNider Hall
Chapel Hill, NC 27599-7000
(919) 962-8331
AMCAS · Deadline: Nov 15 · Public

North Dakota
Univ. of North Dakota School of Medicine
Secretary, Committee on Admissions
501 North Columbia Road, Box 9037
Grand Forks, ND 58202-9037
(701) 777-4221
Deadline: Nov 1 · Public

Ohio
Case Western Reserve School of Medicine
Assoc. Dean for Admissions & Student Affairs
10900 Euclid Avenue
Cleveland, OH 44106-4920
(216) 368-3450
AMCAS · Deadline: Oct 15 · Private

Univ. of Cincinnati College of Medicine
Office of Student Affairs/Admissions
P.O. Box 670552
Cincinnati, OH 45267-0552
(513) 558-7314
AMCAS · Deadline: Nov 15 · Public

Medical College of Ohio
Admissions Office
P.O. Box 10008
Toledo, OH 43699
(419) 383-4229
AMCAS · Deadline: Nov 1 · Public

Northeastern Ohio Univ. College of Medicine
Office of Admissions & Educational Research
P.O. Box 95
Rootstown, OH 44272-0095
(216) 325-2511
AMCAS · Deadline: Nov 1 · Public

Ohio State U. College of Medicine & Public Health
Admissions Committee, 270-A Meiling Hall
370 West Ninth Avenue
Columbus, OH 43210-1238
(614) 292-7137
AMCAS · Deadline: Nov 1 · Public

Wright State Univ. School of Medicine
Office of Student Affairs/Admissions
P.O. Box 1751
Dayton, OH 45401
(513) 873-2934
AMCAS · Deadline: Nov 15 · Public

Oklahoma
Univ. of Oklahoma College of Medicine
P.O. Box 26901
Oklahoma City, OK 73190
(405) 271-2331
AMCAS · Deadline: Oct 15 · Public

Oregon
Oregon Health Sciences U. School of Medicine
Office of Education & Student Affairs, L102
3181 SW Sam Jackson Park Road
Portland, OR 97201
(503) 494-2998
AMCAS · Deadline: Oct 15 · Public

Pennsylvania
Allegheny Univ. of the Health Sciences
MCP-Hahnemann School of Medicine
Admissions Office
2900 Queen Lane Avenue
Philadelphia, PA 19129
(215) 991-8202
AMCAS · Deadline: Dec 1 · Private

Jefferson Medical College
Associate Dean for Admissions
1025 Walnut Street
Philadelphia, PA 19107
(215) 955-6983
AMCAS · Deadline: Nov 15 · Private

Pennsylvania State Univ. College of Medicine
Office of Student Affairs
P.O. Box 850
Hershey, PA 17033
(717) 531-8755
AMCAS · Deadline: Nov 15 · Private

Univ. of Pennsylvania School of Medicine
Director of Admissions and Financial Aid
Edward J. Stemmler Hall, Suite 100
Philadelphia, PA 19104-6056
(215) 898-8001
AMCAS • Deadline: Nov 1 • Private

Univ. of Pittsburgh School of Medicine
Office of Admissions
518 Scaife Hall
Pittsburgh, PA 15261
(412) 648-9891
AMCAS • Deadline: Dec 1 • Private

Temple Univ. School of Medicine
Admissions Office
Suite 305, Student Faculty Center
Broad and Ontario Streets
Philadelphia, PA 19140
(215) 707-3656
AMCAS • Deadline: Dec 1 • Private

Puerto Rico
Univ. Central Del Caribe School of Medicine
Office of Admissions
Ramon Ruiz Arnau Univ. Hospital
Call Box 60-327
Bayamon, PR 00960-6032
(787) 740-1611, ext. 210
AMCAS • Deadline: Dec 15 • Private

Ponce School of Medicine
Admissions Office
P.O. Box 7004
Ponce, PR 00732
(787) 840-2511
AMCAS • Deadline: Dec 15 • Private

Univ. of Puerto Rico School of Medicine
Central Admissions Office
Medical Sciences Campus
P.O. Box 365067
San Juan, PR 00936-5067
(787) 758-2525, ext. 5213
AMCAS • Deadline: Dec 1 • Public

Rhode Island
Brown Univ. School of Medicine
Office of Admissions and Financial Aid
97 Waterman St., Box G-A212
Providence, RI 02912-9706
(401) 863-2149
Deadline: Mar 1 • Private

South Carolina
Medical U. of S. Carolina College of Medicine
Office of Enrollment Services
171 Ashley Avenue
Charleston, SC 29425
(803) 792-3283
AMCAS • Deadline: Dec 1 • Public

Univ. of South Carolina School of Medicine
Associate Dean for Student Programs
Columbia, SC 29208
(803) 733-3325
AMCAS • Deadline: Dec 1 • Public

South Dakota
Univ. of South Dakota School of Medicine
Office of Student Affairs, Room 105
1400 W 22nd St.
Sioux Falls, SD 57105
(605) 357-1422
AMCAS • Deadline: Nov 15 • Public

Tennessee
East Tennessee State Univ.
James H. Quillen College of Medicine
Assistant Dean for Admissions and Records
P.O. Box 70580
Johnson City, TN 37614-0580
(423) 439-6221
AMCAS • Deadline: Dec 1 • Public

Meharry Medical College School of Medicine
Director, Admissions and Records
1005 D. B. Todd Boulevard
Nashville, TN 37208
(615) 327-6223
AMCAS • Deadline: Dec 15 • Private

Univ. of Tennessee College of Medicine
790 Madison Avenue
Memphis, TN 38163-2166
(901) 448-5559
AMCAS • Deadline: Nov 15 • Public

Vanderbilt School of Medicine
Office of Admissions
209 Light Hall
Nashville, TN 37232-0685
(615) 322-2145
AMCAS • Deadline: Oct 15 • Private

Texas
Baylor College of Medicine
Office of Admissions
One Baylor Plaza
Houston, TX 77030
(713) 798-4842
Deadline: Nov 1 • Private

Texas A & M Univ. College of Medicine
Assoc. Dean for Student Affairs & Admissions
College Station, TX 77843-1114
(409) 845-7743
AMCAS • Deadline: Nov 1 • Public

Texas Tech Univ. School of Medicine
Health Sciences Center
Office of Admissions
Lubbock, TX 79430
(806) 743-2297
Deadline: Nov 1 • Public

Univ. of Texas—Galveston Medical Branch
Office of Admissions
G.210, Ashbel Smith Bldg.
Galveston, TX 77555-1317
(409) 772-3517
UTSMDAC • Deadline: Oct 15 • Public

Univ. of Texas—Houston Medical School
Office of Admissions, Room G-024
P.O. Box 20708
Houston, TX 77225
(713) 500-5116
UTSMDAC • Deadline: Oct 15 • Public

Univ. of Texas—San Antonio Medical School
Medical School Admissions/Registrar's Office
Health Science Center
7703 Floyd Curl Drive
San Antonio, TX 78284-7701
(210) 567-2665
UTSMDAC • Deadline: Oct 15 • Public

Univ. of Texas—Southwestern Medical School
Office of the Registrar
5323 Harry Hines Blvd.
Dallas, TX 75235-9096
(214) 648-5617
UTSMDAC • Deadline: Oct 15 • Public

Utah
Univ. of Utah School of Medicine
Director, Medical School Admissions
50 North Medical Drive
Salt Lake City, UT 84132
(801) 581-7498
AMCAS • Deadline: Oct 15 • Public

Vermont
Univ. of Vermont College of Medicine
Admissions Office
C-225 Given Bldg.
Burlington, VT 05405
(802) 656-2154
AMCAS • Deadline: Nov 15 • Public

Virginia
Eastern Virginia Medical School
Office of Admissions
721 Fairfax Avenue
Norfolk, VA 23507-2000
(757) 446-5812
AMCAS • Deadline: Nov 15 • Private

Virginia Commonwealth U. School of Medicine
Medical School Admissions
MCV Station Box 980565
Richmond, VA 23298-0565
(804) 828-9629
AMCAS • Deadline: Nov 15 • Public

Univ. of Virginia School of Medicine
Medical School Admissions Office
Box 235
Charlottesville, VA 22908
(804) 924-5571
AMCAS • Deadline: Nov 1 • Public

Washington
Univ. of Washington School of Medicine
Admissions Office
Health Sciences Center A-300, Box 356340
Seattle, WA 98195
(206) 543-7212
AMCAS • Deadline: Nov 1 • Public

West Virginia
Marshall Univ. School of Medicine
Admissions Office
1542 Spring Valley Drive
Huntington, WV 25704
(304) 696-7312
AMCAS • Deadline: Nov 15 • Public

West Virginia Univ. School of Medicine
Office of Admissions and Records
Health Sciences Center
P.O. Box 9815
Morgantown, WV 26506
(304) 293-3521
AMCAS • Deadline: Nov 15 • Public

Wisconsin
Medical College of Wisconsin
Office of Admissions and Registrar
8701 Watertown Plank Road
Milwaukee, WI 53226
(414) 456-8246
AMCAS • Deadline: Nov 1 • Private

Univ. of Wisconsin Medical School
Admissions Committee
Medical Sciences Center, Room 1250
1300 University Avenue
Madison, WI 53706
(608) 263-4925
AMCAS • Deadline: Oct. 15 • Public

More Great Books from Mustang Publishing

The Complete Book of Golf Games by Scott Johnston. Want to spice up your next round of 18 holes? With over 80 great betting games, side wagers, and tournament formats, this book will delight both weekend hackers and the totally obsessed. From descriptions of favorites like Skins and Nassau to details on unusual contests like String and Bingo Bango Bongo, it's essential equipment in every golfer's bag. **$12.00** *"A must acquisition."*—Petersen's Golfing

How to Be a Way Cool Grandfather by Verne Steen. There are some things a grandfather just ought to know: how to make slingshot from an old limb and a rubber band, how to make a kite from a newspaper, how to do a few simple magic tricks, and how to make his grandchildren say, "Cool, Grandpa!" With complete details on making 30 fun, inexpensive toys, plus hints on using them to impart valuable lessons to kids, this is a great book for every old fogey who'd rather be way cool. **$12.95** *"A fun read…wonderfully presented."*—Tucson Citizen

The Complete Book of Beer Drinking Games by Andy Griscom, Ben Rand, & Scott Johnston. With over 500,000 copies sold, this book reigns as the imbiber's bible! From classic beer games like Quarters and Blow Pong to wild creations like Slush Fund and Beer Hunter—plus funny essays, cartoons, and lists—this book is a party essential! **$8.95** *"The 'Animal House' of literature!"*—Dallas Morning News

Beer Games 2: The Exploitative Sequel by Griscom, Rand, Johnston, & Balay. Here's a sequel that's better than the original! With over 40 great new beer games, more witty essays and lists, and the wacky Beer Catalog, this is a hilarious tribute to beer, college, and the party animal lifestyle. **$8.95** *"Awesome."*—Vermont Cynic

Europe for Free by Brian Butler. If you travel on a tight budget—or if you just love a bargain—this is the book for you! With thousands of things to do and see for free all over Europe, you'll save lots of lira, francs, and pfennigs. **$10.95** *"Well-organized and packed with ideas."*—Modern Maturity

Also in this series:
London for Free ($9.95) • **DC for Free** ($9.95) • **Paris for Free** ($10.95) • **Hawaii for Free** ($9.95) • **The Southwest for Free** ($9.95)

....

Mustang Publishing books should be available in your local bookstore. If not, send a check or money order for the price of the book, plus $3.00 postage per book, to Mustang Publishing, P.O. Box 770426, Memphis, TN 38177 USA. To order by credit card, call toll free 800-250-8713 (or 901-684-1200).

Allow three weeks for delivery. For rush, one-week delivery, add $2.00 to the total. International orders: Please pay in U.S. funds, and add $5.00 to the total for Air Mail.

For a complete catalog of Mustang Publishing books, send $2.00 and a stamped, self-addressed, business-size envelope to Catalog Request, Mustang Publishing, P.O. Box 770426, Memphis, TN 38177 USA.